West, Samuel Gregg argues, was not just science, politics, or economics, but a vision of the human person that did not separate but integrated faith and reason. Gregg shows the way out of our spreading 'pathologies of reason and faith,' demonstrating the true nature, and limitations, of reason, its deep connection to faith, and their complementary roles. The benefits of Western civilization can be realized in no other way. Gregg shows us how they might be preserved not only for us but for future generations."

—**James R. Otteson,** Thomas W. Smith Presidential Chair in Business Ethics, professor of economics at Wake Forest University

"Faith and reason form the foundation of the optimistic outlook in Samuel Gregg's book. He shows how reason unmoored in faith and faith detached from reason easily drift into forms of unequal treatment, denying our creation in the image of God, which anchors us in hope. From Genesis to Paul, Gregg shows that the arrow is from Truth to Freedom, through *logos* to 'enlightenment.' The West has flourished in this freedom. May it *never* be lost."

—**Vernon L. Smith,** 2002 Nobel laureate in Economics, Chapman University

"Samuel Gregg has written a clear, eloquent, and concise guide to the intellectual and spiritual currents, rooted in reason and faith, which inform Western civilization at its best. He does full justice to the West's Jewish and Christian roots and their affirmation of reason's ability to articulate freedom's purposes. He also lauds the best currents of Enlightenment thought even as he warns against the 'forces of destruction' that increasingly impel the modern world toward tyranny and a soul-destroying nihilism. With impressive learning and grace, he shows his readers 'a way back' to the old verities that point the way toward a promising future. A must-read for all who care about the fate of a Western civilization rooted in truth and liberty."

—**Daniel J. Mahoney,** Assumption College, author of *The Idol of Our Age: How the Religion of Humanity Subverts Christianity*

Reason, Faith, and the Struggle for Western Civilization

Reason, Faith, *and the* Struggle *for* Western Civilization

SAMUEL GREGG

REGNERY GATEWAY

Regnery Gateway™ is a trademark of Salem Communications Holding Corporation
Regnery® is a registered trademark of Salem Communications Holding Corporation

Cataloging-in-Publication data on file with the Library of Congress

ISBN 978-1-62157-802-4
ebook ISBN 978-1-62157-906-9

Published in the United States by
Regnery Publishing
A Division of Salem Media Group
300 New Jersey Ave NW
Washington, DC 20001
www.Regnery.com

Manufactured in the United States of America

10 9 8 7 6 5 4 3 2 1

Books are available in quantity for promotional or premium use. For information on discounts and terms, please visit our website: www.Regnery.com.

For Madeleine

Madame,
Reason is our soul's left hand, Faith her right,
By these we reach divinity . . .
—*John Donne*

Contents

Preface

The theme of this book has long occupied my mind. I have reflected upon it in various settings for more than a decade. Over that period, nothing has changed my view that the primary challenge facing what we call the West is neither political nor economic. Economics and politics matter. But I have become convinced that the most important questions facing Western societies logically precede these topics and, in many respects, predetermine how we address them.

The ways in which the relation between reason and faith has shaped the West, for better and for worse, are in many ways subterranean. Occasionally, however, they thrust themselves directly into our view.

One such manifestation was the religiously associated violence that Western nations confronted during the first two decades of the twenty-first century. I hope, however, that this book shows that the far greater bloodshed of the twentieth century's darkest decades, carried out at the behest of ideologies that hardly need to be named, owed much to what I call, after Joseph Ratzinger, pathologies of reason and faith.

Fortunately, there is more to this story than the ways in which Western societies become unmoored whenever reason and faith drift away from each other. One argument of this book is that not only can reason and faith correct each other's excesses, but they can also enhance each other's comprehension of the truth, continually renewing Western civilization.

I am also convinced that the various movements of ideas and persons often grouped together under that catchall term the "Enlightenment" need not be perpetually at odds with what I regard as the religions of the West.

It isn't a question of ignoring tensions. They abound and are noted throughout this book. But the ideas that began emerging toward the end of the seventeenth century are inexplicable without the background of the Jewish and Christian faiths and cultures out of which the Enlightenment arose. Likewise, more than a few of the freedoms and achievements now embraced by believing Jews and Christians would have struggled to see the light of day without the efforts of certain figures associated with the Enlightenment.

If this book dismantles several myths about the Enlightenment's relation to the faiths of the West and demonstrates that reason and faith need not be locked in an endless struggle for supremacy, it will have achieved more than I could hope. There is no going back to a pre-Enlightenment world. But we need not settle for a civilization shaped by an Enlightenment that marginalizes Jewish and Christian faith.

All books reflect the ideas that have influenced their authors. This book has its roots in the thought of two scholars who draw upon modern and premodern intellectual traditions. One is the aforementioned Joseph Ratzinger. The other is John Finnis. I continue to learn from their erudition and writings. Other thinkers whose contributions have shaped specific sections of this text include Father Samir Khalil Samir, S.J., Vernon L. Smith, and the late Michael Novak.

These men have labored in quite different fields, and some readers may be uncertain about the field to which this book belongs. I do not think, however, that a single disciplinary outlook could capture the manifold ways in which the interaction, development, and clash of ideas about reason and faith have molded and periodically disrupted the West's cultural, moral, legal, and economic history. But if this book must be classified, let it be called a history of ideas.

This text also reflects some more immediate debts. The first of these is to Regnery Publishing's Gateway imprint and Thomas Spence for commissioning this project. My hope is that the book embodies the intellectual rigor and spirit of discovery that this imprint aims to realize.

The second is to those publishing outlets where I have previously written about some of the themes addressed in this book. These include *Public Discourse*, *Library of Law and Liberty*, *Catholic World Report*, and *The Stream*, which kindly granted me permission to draw upon several essays that I have penned for them.

Much of this book was written in America. Parts of it, however, were composed in locations ranging from Rome and Jerusalem to Aberdeenshire, Santiago, and Sydney. There could be few better reminders that the West is more than geography and of the universal meaning of its civilizational character.

Finally, a note about the dedication: it is to my daughter, the one I hope will experience the fullness of life in a civilization that will overcome its present traumas and regain the confidence to allow itself to be nourished by *ratio* and *fides*—always together and never apart.

CHAPTER ONE

The Speech That Shook the World

Faith certainly tells us what the senses do not, but not the
contrary of what they see; it is above, not against them.
—Blaise Pascal

L ocated about sixty miles north of Munich, the small Bavarian
city of Regensburg was the site of a Roman garrison from the
end of the first century AD. You can still see the Porta Prae-
toria (Praetorian Gate) constructed by Emperor Marcus Aurelius in
the second century to defend a major point of entry into the Roman
Empire. For centuries afterwards, Regensburg served as a crossroads
of European trade. It was also a seat of the Holy Roman Empire's
parliament, the site of a massacre of Jews by Crusaders making their
way east to seize back control of the Holy Land from Muslim invaders, and the site of a major battle during the Napoleonic Wars.

Among Regensburg's most famous inhabitants have been the
Jewish mystic Judah ben Samuel (1150–1217) and one of the
greatest minds of the Middle Ages, Albertus Magnus (1200–
1280), the patron saint of natural scientists and bishop of the
city for three years.

Modernization came after World War II with the arrival of state-of-the-art factories employing hundreds of people and the establishment, in 1965, of the University of Regensburg. One of the first faculties to hold classes was that of Catholic Theology. Its star recruit arrived in 1969, a forty-two-year-old native Bavarian, Father Joseph Ratzinger, who had made a name for himself as a theologian advising Catholic bishops during the Second Vatican Council (1962–1965).

Returning to his old university on September 12, 2006, Ratzinger, now Pope Benedict XVI, delivered a lecture bearing the seemingly harmless title "Faith, Reason, and the University: Memories and Reflections" to old friends and the Regensburg faculty.

Hours later, the world exploded.

An emperor speaks

Across the globe, Pope Benedict's lecture was ferociously attacked by Muslim religious and political leaders. In several Muslim countries, there were mass rallies and riots, some of which culminated in attacks on Christian churches. Most terribly, an Italian nun, Sister Leonella Sgorbati, and her Muslim driver, Mohamed Osman Mohamud, were gunned down by two jihadists outside a children's hospital in Somalia, five days after Benedict's Regensburg address.

Few of those chanting their fury at the pope, I suspect, had actually read Benedict's words. What had enraged some Muslims was his quotation from a Byzantine emperor's dialogue with an unnamed Persian from around the year 1391.[1]

The emperor Manuel II Palaeologus (1350–1425) was that rare combination of politician, soldier, and scholarly author of poetry and theological treatises. Having spent much of his youth as a hostage at the court of the Ottoman sultan Bayezid I, he was familiar with Muslim thought and practice.² In his dialogue with the Persian, Manuel focused on Islam's long and disconcerting history of invoking religious claims to justify violence. Violence, the emperor frankly stated, seemed endemic in the Muslim world. "Show me," he wrote in the passage quoted by Benedict at Regensburg, "just what Mohammed brought about that was new, and there you will find things only evil and inhuman, such as his command to spread by the sword the faith he preached."³

The frenzied nature of some Muslims' reaction to this quotation—and the constant invocation of the Koran by jihadists such as those who had destroyed the Twin Towers in New York five years and one day before the Regensburg lecture—convinced many Westerners that this Byzantine emperor was onto something. After all, people who take reason seriously don't respond to criticism with insults, threats, or violence.

The fury provoked by Benedict's speech, however, distracted attention from the pope's central point about religion's place in the West and faith's relation to something regarded as essential to the West's identity—*reason*.

The Regensburg lecture certainly concerned Islam, reminding Westerners that the problem of jihadist terrorism was at its root theological. That was an unwelcome message to the many Westerners convinced that poverty is the cause of most problems and unwilling to acknowledge that different understandings of God can have different practical consequences—for better or for worse.

Is God a reasonable Deity? This question *matters*, not least because one alternative to a Deity who embodies reason is a Deity who is pure will, operating beyond reason. Quoting the French scholar of Islam, Roger Arnaldez, Benedict noted in his Regensburg lecture that such a God "is not bound even by his own word." He could even command us "to practice idolatry."⁴

It requires little imagination to realize that such a God *could* bless flying passenger planes into skyscrapers or cutting the throat of an eighty-five-year-old priest as he celebrates Mass in his parish church in France.

The significance of Benedict's remarks thus extended far beyond Islam. His lecture was about *us*, we who have inherited the civilization called the West. His question to everyone who thinks that Western civilization is worth preserving and promoting—a question that is central to this book—was this: Do *you* understand that unless the West gets the relation between reason and faith right, it will be unable to overcome its inner traumas or defend itself from those who wage war against it in the name of particular ideologies?

In answering this question, my objective is not to produce an exhaustive study of the ideas that have shaped the West, nor do I try to assess the effects of every major historical event or epoch on the relation between reason and faith. I am certainly not proposing that all the West's problems revolve around the question raised at Regensburg. Mono-causal explanations are usually wrong.

Instead I want to show how the expression and makeover of different ideas about reason and faith by such figures as Plato, the Hebrew prophets, the apostle Paul, Thomas Aquinas, Karl Marx, John Stuart Mill, and Friedrich Nietzsche have contributed to civilizational growth but also regression in the West.

Through an examination of these and other thinkers, we'll see how the West's unique integration of reason and faith—specifically, Jewish and Christian faith—encouraged the ideas, commitments, and institutions that give the West its core identity. But we'll also observe how mistaken conceptions of reason and faith have enabled the emergence of intellectual movements such as scientism, Marxism, and Nietzscheanism—and more recent phenomena like liberal religion, authoritarian relativism, and Islamism—which corrode and threaten those same ideas, commitments, and institutions.[5]

Defining the West

At this point, readers will start asking important questions. What is the West? When did the West begin? How does it differ from other civilizations? Who is a Westerner? What's so special about the West that it is worth defending? Does the West mean anything anymore?

Western civilization began in the Mediterranean basin, from which it spread. Today, it tends to be associated with North America and Europe, particularly Western Europe, regions that remained relatively free and democratic during the Cold War. Communist regimes were seen as standing for totalitarianism, economic collectivism, and deep hostility to the two faiths of the West, Judaism and Christianity.

A moment's thought, however, makes it clear that Western civilization can't be primarily about geography, including that of the Cold War. Did Poland cease to be part of the West because it was governed by Marxist-Leninists between 1947 and 1989? Would anyone suggest that Australia, Uruguay, New Zealand, Chile, or Israel isn't part of the West simply because it is not in North America or Europe?

Trying to define the West geographically becomes even more difficult when we consider that some countries reflect mixtures of civilizational influences. Lebanon, for example, is deeply marked by various expressions of Islam and Arab culture. Thanks, however, to Christianity's two-thousand-year presence there and the nation's enduring links to France, it's plausible to describe Lebanon as more Western than, say, Saudi Arabia, even though Beirut is closer to Riyadh than to London.

We move onto firmer ground when we start identifying cultural accomplishments that can only be described as Western. No one would mistake the Parthenon, the Rule of St. Benedict, Michelangelo's *David*, Mozart's *Coronation Mass*, Plato's *Gorgias*, Jefferson's Monticello, Bach's *Brandenburg Concertos*, the United States Constitution, or Shakespeare's *Richard III* as representative of Japanese, Persian, Tibetan, or Thai culture.

Another way of understanding the West is through such representative figures as Charlemagne, Alexis de Tocqueville, Theodor Herzl, Galileo Galilei, Charles de Gaulle, John Locke, Jane Austen, Christopher Columbus, Ludwig van Beethoven, Marie Curie, Czesław Miłosz, Albert Einstein, Flannery O'Connor, Voltaire, Golda Meir, or George Washington. These people belong to different historical periods and held dissimilar views on many questions. But would we view any of them as rooted in Hindi civilization or any of the numerous African cultures?

Many of these figures also consciously thought of themselves as belonging to the West. The biographer Jean Lacouture writes that Charles de Gaulle "had a clear idea not only of France but of Western civilization, and in 1939 he was never in any doubt as to his duty to confront the challenge thrown down by totalitarianism."[6] Something similar can be said of de Gaulle's most important wartime ally, Winston Churchill, who understood on the eve of the Battle of Britain that "the survival of Christian civilization" was at stake.[7]

For de Gaulle and Churchill, the fight against National Socialism was not about protecting a localized portion of human history. It was about saving universal aspirations and achievements of concern to *all* humanity.

Threats have a way of concentrating the mind. They cause us to ask ourselves what we are willing to fight and perhaps even die for. In the twentieth century, the twin totalitarianisms of Nazism and

Communism had that effect. People had to consider what the West *really* stood for and *why* these ideologies were antithetical to Western civilization, even though fascism and Marxism were products of Western minds.

This pushes us to clarify which ideas are distinctly Western, to identify those that have contributed to the West's development as a civilization, and to specify how they differ from other cultures' dominant intellectual settings.

Take, for instance, political ideas such as personal freedom, the rule of law, constitutionally limited government, the distinction between church and state, and human rights. Few would dispute that these concepts have received their fullest expression in Western societies. When we speak of nations "Westernizing," we mean they are adopting ideas such as these.

Rationality and religion

Many societies outside Europe and North America have adopted Western institutions and even particular Western ideas. But does this mean all of them have become Western?

After 1853, Japan reversed almost two hundred years of attempted isolationism and began embracing Western technology and political structures. The Meiji Restoration, as it came to be called, also involved extensive industrialization. Today, terms like "democratic," "economically developed," and even "modern" can rightly be applied to Japan.

But most people, including most Japanese, would pause before describing Japan as a Western country. That hesitation surely has something to do with Japanese *culture*. Even after more than 150 years of sustained interaction with Western countries, Japanese culture remains distinct from that of Poland, Spain, or Canada. An important reason for this distinction is that the Meiji reformers weren't interested in turning Japan into a *Western* nation. They certainly wanted to transform the economy, employ modern technology, and develop Japan's ability to defend itself against other nation-states. Nonetheless, the Meiji reformers also insisted on grounding these changes in traditional Japanese values.[8]

Another example of modernization without Westernization is the reforms embarked upon by the Ottoman Empire from the 1840s onwards. While commonly described as an exercise in Westernization and secularization, twenty-first-century scholars have established that successive Ottoman governments adopted Western technology, military methods, and administrative methods without fully embracing Western principles. Instead, as one historian of the Middle East observes, they consistently associated their reform efforts with "Islam, the sultan and caliph, the glories of the Ottoman and Islamic past, and the anxiously hoped-for return to splendor and worldly power."[9]

"Modernization" and "Westernization," then, are not the same thing. It is possible to embrace institutions or technologies developed in the West without embracing Western culture in its totality.

The term "culture" is derived from the Latin word *cultus*, meaning that which is adorned, cultivated, protected, and worshipped. If, then, we want to understand what is central to a civilization's culture, we must ask what it seeks to uphold. What does it revere? What "cult" is at its heart?

For centuries, the West has attached great value to *freedom*. The nineteenth-century historian Lord Acton famously portrayed Western history as the movement, in fits and starts, from oppression towards liberty, understood as the minimization of unreasonable constraints. "Liberty," he wrote, "is the delicate fruit of a mature civilization."[10] Even Marx saw the end-state of history, which he called Communism, as a world in which everyone would be free "to do one thing today and another tomorrow; to hunt in the morning, fish in the afternoon, breed cattle in the evening and criticize after dinner, just as [one] please[s]."[11]

This concern with freedom can be found as far back as the Greek encounter with the empires of Asia. Toward the end of his conquest of the Persian Empire, Alexander the Great started adopting Persian customs, particularly the practice of *proskynesis*, the prostration of a subject before the monarch. The historian Arrian records that many of Alexander's officers criticized his espousal of *proskynesis*. Greeks regarded such submission as due only to the gods. Associating the practice with Eastern despotism, they regarded it as unworthy of free men.[12]

But *why* has the ideal of liberty been so central to the growth of the West? Why did the Greek states that resisted the Persian Empire's drive for transcontinental hegemony regard themselves as combatting despotism? I think that this emphasis on freedom is derived from something even more central to Western civilization—*the commitment to reasoned inquiry in search of truth*.

The exercise of reason is found in all societies. Numerous cultures have recognized that it distinguishes man from other creatures. Even so, the emphasis on the mind's ability to apprehend truth—and not only scientific truths but also philosophical and religious truths—is woven into the intellectual fabric of the West.

Consider the philosophical accomplishments that grew out of Socratic thought, or the Romans' clarification of legal relationships, or the effort of medieval and modern thinkers to apply the scientific method to the physical world. To varying degrees, each of these endeavors reflects a suspicion of superstition, mistrust of arbitrary power, a desire to avoid error, a conviction that communities should be just, and a concern for freedom.

These ideas took centuries to develop in Western societies, with many detours and reversals along the way. Elements of them are discernible in other cultures. Still, a strong association between a concern to act reasonably, the growth of freedom, and the establishment of justice is apparent in the West as long ago as Socrates's unwillingness to support the Athenian oligarchy's unjust execution of Leon of Salamis.

Even European princes such as France's Louis XIV, who aimed at absolute rule, tried to evade accusations of despotism. Arbitrary government, they knew, was regarded as unjust and therefore risked generating strong opposition, as Charles I of England eventually learned. The same principles permit us to classify National Socialist and Communist systems as antithetical to Western civilization precisely because such regimes subordinated freedom, the good, justice, and rationality itself to the requirements of "the master race," "the will to power," or "the dictatorship of the proletariat."

We should also recall that Western culture has never reduced liberty or justice to the eradication of unjust coercion. Western thinkers from Plato to James Madison have maintained the substantive distinction between opting to spend one's life in a drug-induced stupor and using one's mind and freedom to improve oneself and the political, legal, and economic order. The first choice is for depravity, the second is for civilization.

Western civilization has thus emphasized what the theologian Servais Pinckaers called freedom for excellence.[13] The West's fullest idea of liberty is consequently what Edward Gibbon called "rational freedom"—a state of affairs in which our passions are ruled by our reason.[14]

This strong attachment to reason, however, does not by itself account for the distinctive character of the West. Without the Christian and Jewish religions, there is no Ambrose, Benedict, Aquinas, Maimonides, Hildegard of Bingen, Isaac Abravanel, Thomas More, Elizabeth of Hungary, John Calvin, Ignatius of Loyola, Hugo Grotius,

John Witherspoon, William Wilberforce, Søren Kierkegaard, Fyodor Dostoyevsky, C. S. Lewis, Edith Stein, Elizabeth Anscombe, Reformation, Oxford University, Caravaggio's *Calling of Saint Matthew*, Bach's *Saint John Passion*, Dante's *Divine Comedy*, Pascal's *Pensées*, Hagia Sophia, Mont-Saint-Michel, or Rome's Great Synagogue. Absent the vision of God articulated first by Judaism and then infused into the West's marrow by Christianity, it's harder to imagine developments like the delegitimization of slavery or the de-deification of the state and the natural world.

The correct response to Tertullian's famous question—"What has Athens to do with Jerusalem?"—is *everything*. And this isn't just because these clearly Western men and women and works can't be separated from Judaism or Christianity.

The first book of the canon of both religions, Genesis, calls upon man to unfold the potentiality in God's original creative act, thereby encouraging human creativity and impatience with passivity. Likewise, the idea that all men are equal *qua* men acquired exceptional force thanks to Judaism's and Christianity's stress that all men are made in the image of God. Similarly, the concept of liberty—in the sense that God leaves man "in the hand of his own counsel" *and* urges him freely to choose to transcend moral mediocrity—is outlined in biblical texts ranging from Ecclesiasticus 15:14 to Galatians 5:1.

The biblical emphasis on freedom is balanced by the insistence that human beings are not God and that they are constantly tempted to use their reason wrongly. This recognition of the limits of reason reinforced the Western emphasis on limiting state power and generated resistance to the utopian urges that have intermittently surfaced throughout Western history.

Undergirding this religious outlook is the recognition that God's true nature is not revealed in beliefs that posit nothingness as illumination or in religions populated by the frivolous and all-too-human gods of Rome and Greece, or creeds that require absolute submission to a Divine Will who can order us to act unreasonably. Instead we find a God of love *and* divine reason. We discover that at the beginning of everything created there is not chaos but *Logos*, an idea to which we will return.

What went wrong?

This brings us face-to-face with a problem that any discussion of Western civilization is bound to encounter: the West has been the source of ideas and movements that *contradict* both reason and key Jewish and Christian teachings.

The ideologies that inflicted the mass slaughters of the twentieth century didn't originate in Asia or Africa. The beliefs underlying Communism and Nazism were developed and expounded by people who would not have thought of themselves as anything but Western. That includes men like Marx and Friedrich Engels as well as such intellectual forebears of Nazism as the Anglo-German philosopher of race Houston Stewart Chamberlain and the French political theorist Arthur de Gobineau. These men grew up in Western societies, had Western educations, and were well-versed in the Western canon.

Nor is it difficult to find examples of Westerners engaging in seriously evil actions. Many of the men responsible for *the* event which led many to question Western civilization's very integrity—the Holocaust—were ostensibly rational, upper-middle-class men who had studied in universities in a country that regarded itself as an advanced culture.

Why did these men end up following a poorly educated Austrian drifter? How could they have believed that it was their duty to wipe an entire people off the face of the earth? What led a sophisticated Western society to embrace a genocidal regime?

Similar questions can be asked about another group of very bright persons, typically regarded as far more benign in their inspiration and activities: the American Progressives.

The word "progress" conjures up images of enlightened persons selflessly battling bigotry and ignorance. Under the influence of ideas that thrived in late-nineteenth-century German universities and often motivated by liberal Protestantism's Social Gospel, the Progressives exerted considerable influence upon American universities, politics, culture, and economic policy from the late nineteenth century onward.

A common trait of the Progressives was their skepticism about the seemingly chaotic workings of America's experiment in ordered liberty. Lawyers such as Justice Felix Frankfurter, ministers of religion like the Congregationalist pastor Washington Gladden, economists such as Richard T. Ely, efficiency experts like the engineer Frederick Winslow Taylor, and politicians such as President Woodrow Wilson believed they knew better.

Most people regard Progressivism as the intellectual force that drove the state's expansion in pursuit of specific social and economic goals in America. But Progressivism had another, more sinister, side.

In his book *Illiberal Reformers: Race, Eugenics, and American Economics in the Progressive Era* (2016), Thomas C. Leonard shows that Progressivism was heavily influenced by two particularly insidious ideologies. The first was eugenics, the idea that humanity's "genetic health" could be protected from "bad breeding" and even enhanced by purposeful social selection. The second was race science, which asserted that different races were intrinsically unequal in abilities. Race science relied heavily on nineteenth-century polygenism, the theory, now generally rejected, that men developed out of several independent pairs of ancestors.

Eugenics and race science are commonly associated with the policies of Nazi Germany, such as the 1935 Nuremburg race laws and the regime's efforts to sterilize (beginning in 1934) and euthanize (beginning in 1939) the mentally and physically impaired. But Leonard points out that eugenics and race science were also "politically influential, culturally fashionable, and scientifically mainstream" in non-Catholic Western countries for at least fifty years.[15]

These ideas influenced many policies advocated by Progressives. Reason and science, they believed, had opened the way to identify the fittest, whom government should favor through specific marriage, reproduction, labor, and immigration policies.[16] In 1911, Woodrow Wilson, then the governor of New Jersey, signed legislation forcing sterilization on what eugenicists regarded as "the hopelessly defective and criminal classes."[17] Other Progressives wanted health care for black Americans to implement eugenic measures to improve the "quality" and diminish the number of black births.[18]

Race science likewise permeated Progressive thought and policies. Wilson's monumental *History of the American People* asserted that southern and eastern Europeans had "neither skill nor energy nor any initiative of quick intelligence."[19] Such thinking inspired measures such as minimum-wage laws designed to exclude from the labor market Asian or Jewish migrants who might drag down the wages of supposedly more industrious Anglo-Saxons.[20]

Women didn't escape the Progressives' dragnet. Sound breeding, they insisted, required that women not work outside the home. Many Progressives saw state-mandated "family wages" as a means of keeping Anglo-Saxon women at home. This, it was hoped, would reverse declining Anglo-Saxon birthrates and protect America from being overrun by "lesser peoples."[21]

These and other views were not universal among Progressives, but their prevalence bespeaks the respectability that these notions achieved throughout the West.[22]

Many other evils could be added to this catalogue of Western sins: slavery, religious persecutions, serfdom, and so on, each of which was at one time regarded as warranted by reason or faith or both.

Those jihadist terrorists who took many lives in Western countries and elsewhere from the early 2000s onwards believed that their acts enjoyed divine warrant. Yet we don't have to look far to find Westerners engaging in equally outrageous acts in the name of ideas that *repudiate* religion.

Between the 1870s and 1920s, Western countries experienced a wave of spectacular terrorist acts committed by self-described anarchists. Besides bombing targets from Wall Street to the Barcelona opera house, they assassinated politically prominent figures like Tsar Alexander II, Empress Elizabeth of Austria-Hungary, Prime Minister Antonio Cánovas del Castillo of Spain, President Marie François Carnot of France, King Umberto I of Italy, and President William McKinley of the United States.

The rise of anarchist terrorism obviously owed much to particular ideas circulating in the late nineteenth century. Prominent among them was the so-called "propaganda of the deed," the belief that the way to bring about radical change was assassinating prominent representatives of the ruling order, demonstrating the fragility of the status quo for the supposedly oppressed masses.

Nor can other evils in Western history be explained without attention to specific, historically contingent factors. Would Hitler have risen to power without the scars left on Germany by World War I? Would the Bolshevik movement have triumphed in Russia without Lenin's sheer ruthlessness? Would eugenics and race science have achieved widespread acceptance in educated Western circles absent Charles Darwin's *Origin of Species* which, whatever its scientific merits, indisputably fed the popularity of these theories?

Nevertheless, the consistent resurfacing of these types of movements and events in Western societies suggests a deeper tension which has long permeated Western culture, one that affects its foundations of reason and faith. Explaining how the failure to master that tension could prove fatal to the West was the purpose of Benedict XVI's Regensburg lecture.

Pathologies of faith, pathologies of reason

The Regensburg lecture wasn't the first occasion on which Joseph Ratzinger had addressed this problem. In a series of articles written before becoming pope, he explored what he called at Regensburg "pathologies of religion and reason."

Throughout these writings, we find numerous references to the "Age of Enlightenment." Popularly associated with modern science and progress, the Enlightenment spirit is perhaps best summarized in the Latin phrase of the German philosopher Immanuel Kant: *sapere aude*—dare to think for yourself! For some people, one inference of this was that religion, especially Christianity, had discouraged entire societies from doing so.

As we shall see in subsequent chapters, the Enlightenment was much more complicated and far less monolithic than is often realized. It wasn't a single episode, a set of accomplishments, or even the discovery of a single way forward. Nor was it anywhere nearly as antireligious as is sometimes supposed. For the moment, it is sufficient to say that groups of thinkers and public figures in the West throughout the late seventeenth and the eighteenth centuries began self-consciously to regard themselves as "enlightened" and as living in a time of "enlightenment": a new period of history that everyone had to learn to live "in light of."

A common characteristic of many such men was their sense of hope. The very word "enlighten" suggested the dawn of a happier, more peaceful, less arbitrary world in the here-and-now, a world that, many Enlightenment thinkers believed, might even anticipate what Christianity had long proclaimed to be the eternal happiness of heaven.

Becoming enlightened also meant using human reason to identify various principles in the natural order and employing that knowledge to change the world and humanity itself for the better. This disposition was accompanied by a commitment to applying reason to man's habits of mind, customs, and traditions to assess whether they contributed to his well-being or oppression.

Given his reputation as a "conservative," many are surprised to learn that Ratzinger never expressed hostility, in principle, to any of these developments, let alone the Age of Enlightenment itself. Many of Ratzinger's writings about reason and faith take the various Enlightenments and the world of science as their starting point.

In an essay titled "Faith between Reason and Feeling," Ratzinger reflected upon a conversation that took place in 1927 among three future Nobel Prize-winning physicists: Werner Heisenberg, Wolfgang Pauli, and Paul Dirac. Their subject was Einstein's conception of God and the conviction of another Nobel physicist, Max Planck, that science and religion were not in conflict.[23]

According to Ratzinger, Heisenberg—perhaps most famous as the principal architect of Nazi Germany's effort to build a nuclear weapon—believed that the lack of conflict proceeded from a conviction that science is focused upon what is "true and false." Religion, by contrast, is about "good and bad." Science is "objective." Religion is "subjective" [24]—a matter of "taste," as Friedrich Schleiermacher, the Prussian theologian and father of liberal Christianity, put it.[25]

Ratzinger notes, however, that Heisenberg remained unsure that man could survive this separation of "knowledge and faith." [26] In short, the *scientist*—the Enlightenment figure par excellence—recognized that if faith were primarily concerned with subjective experiences such as emotions, and if knowledge were reduced to what is empirically verifiable, we would have a major problem. Religious beliefs, these physicists understood, are powerful forces. If impervious or hostile to reason, they are potentially very dangerous.

Ratzinger concluded by underscoring Pauli's observation that the division between faith and reason ensures that "things will happen that are more frightful than anything we can yet imagine." In the somber tone of one who had lived through it, Ratzinger commented, "the unholy twelve years would begin" only six years after this conversation occurred.[27]

At no point in any of his engagements with these questions about science and religion did Ratzinger demean the scientific method, the cornerstone of modern inquiry. It entails (1) posing a question, such as "Why is grass green?", (2) developing a hypothesis to explain why grass is green, (3) making predictions about how grass becomes green based on that hypothesis, (4) testing that hypothesis through experiments on grass, and (5) analyzing the experiments' results to see if they fit the hypothesis. If the evidence does not fit the hypothesis, one needs a new hypothesis. If the evidence does fit the hypothesis, one can pose further questions, like "Does chlorophyll's role in making grass green help explain other plants' colors?" This is an example of how, as Ratzinger put it, "Reason that operates in specialized areas...gains enormously in strength and capability." [28]

The problem is that if we reduce reason to the scientific method and limit knowledge to the measurable, science ceases to be guided by what is *morally* reasonable. The door is then opened to horrors such as medical *experiments* on priests in Dachau, the *systematic* use of terror by Communist regimes against their opponents, and the *efficient* destruction of European Jewry.

Part of the difficulty, Ratzinger holds, is that many Enlightenment thinkers did not have *enough* faith in reason. Today, according to Ratzinger, many who take pride in their reasonableness "no longer offer any perspective on the fundamental questions of mankind." [29] Why? Because neither technical expertise nor the natural sciences can explain *why*, for instance, we should want to cure disease or reduce poverty in the first place.

But a similar criticism, Ratzinger carefully adds, applies to some people of faith. Having accepted reason's reduction to the scientific, they sought a new space for religion. "That," he writes, "is why 'feeling' was assigned to [religion] as its own domain within human existence." Here we're reminded of Faust's response to Gretchen's question about the nature of religion: "Feeling is all. The rest is just smoke and mirrors." [30]

The effects of this turn were especially damaging to Christianity precisely because it had long valued reason. Some Christians no longer considered it necessary to "always be ready to give an explanation to anyone who asks you for a reason for your hope" (1 Peter 3:15). But having ceased proposing the reasonableness of Christian faith, other believers started making basic errors in logic. This is exemplified by what is called the historical-critical method for analyzing the Bible, which seeks to discover a text's basic meaning by reconstructing the historical situation of the text's author and readers. Since the nineteenth century, some biblical scholars have seen the historical-critical method as the truly scientific approach and thus the only "real" way to comprehend these writings.

There's no doubt that we've learned much about the Hebrew and Christian scriptures through the historical-critical method. Unfortunately, a more or less exclusive reliance on this method, combined with the unspoken assumption that these texts should be analyzed from the standpoint of unbelief, rules out the reasonable position that it is rational to believe that the miracles of Jesus of Nazareth were real *if* one recognizes that a reasonable God may have good reasons to suspend the laws of nature to attest to the truth about who Christ is.

Christ's miracles are thus quickly reduced to metaphors or "faith-experiences," despite the Gospels' insistence that these were *real* events witnessed by *real* people, *not* stories akin to the Greek myths. Christianity, the Jesuit theologian Jean Daniélou once wrote, is very much faith in a historical *event*—the Resurrection—and historical events are not fictions.[31]

Even more seriously, in reason's absence we can no longer ask whether one religion's claims are more truthful than another's. Nor can we recognize that there are, as Ratzinger wrote in another article, "sick and distorted forms of religion."[32] A faith may be so unreasonable that some of its followers believe it permits them to do terrible things. In other cases, a disdain for reason may lead some Christians to reduce the central figure of Christianity, Jesus of Nazareth, to the equivalent of a celestial teddy bear.

Forward . . . to the past

From this perspective, the external assault on the West by religiously inspired terrorists, the internal crumbling that manifests itself in reason's reduction to science, and faith's collapse into sentimentalism have more in common than we realize. They reflect a lack of confidence in, if not a repudiation of, the relation between faith and reason that has long distinguished Western civilization and provided much of its transformative strength.

To fully comprehend how and why this collapse of confidence happened, we need to understand how the West first integrated faith and reason. We therefore must go back, not, in the first instance, to learned sages in Athens but to a small tribe living in a narrow hilly region bounded by sea and desert on one of the great crossroads of Asia and Africa and of East and West.

Chapter Two

Making the West

The various modes of worship which prevailed in the
Roman world were all considered by the people as equally
true; by the philosophers as equally false; and by the mag-
istrate as equally useful.
—*Edward Gibbon*

I f Isaac Newton has good claim to the title of Britain's greatest
scientist, Edward Gibbon is a contender for its most consequential historian.

That reputation is partly the result of Gibbon's approach to history. He focused rigorously on primary sources and anticipated modern methods such as examining archaeological evidence. But it was
the sheer magnitude of Gibbon's project and his willingness to make
judgments about one of the West's most significant historical developments that made him so influential.

The first volumes of Gibbon's *History of the Decline and Fall of
the Roman Empire* were published in 1776, the year Britain's American colonies declared their independence. The last volumes appeared

in 1788, on the eve of what Europeans for decades afterwards would call "The Revolution."

Like the French Revolution, Rome's decline has long troubled Western minds. While the empire perpetuated errors like slavery, it exemplified a type of unity expressed in the sovereignty of one emperor and a uniform legal code. Above all, being a Roman citizen made one part of a culture distinct from those whom Greeks and Romans called "barbarians." To be Roman was to be civilized. That was the deepest meaning of the phrase *civis romanus sum*.

Civilizational preeminence can be understood in material and scientific terms, but it has always implied more than technological prowess. The Greeks and Romans didn't refer to outsiders as barbarians because of their military inferiority. Educated Greeks and Romans viewed their world as constituting a standard by which to assess other cultures.

To believe such things requires tremendous self-assurance. In the acclaimed 1969 BBC series *Civilisation*, the art historian Kenneth Clark sat in the foreground of an old viaduct and spoke about the Romans' "confidence." He didn't mean arrogance. Clark had in mind the Romans' conviction that the ideas and institutions they had inherited and developed were a singular accomplishment, worthy of emulation.

Exploring why this world eventually fell, Gibbon was attentive to many factors—inept rulers, abuses of power by the Praetorian Guard who protected the imperial family, and the creeping bureaucratization that made it harder for Rome's leaders to adapt to new threats. But one of his primary explanations for the empire's eclipse had less to do with power politics and more to do with culture. In Gibbon's view, Rome suffered from an erosion of classical and military virtues among its elites. They became disinclined to fight to defend the empire, preferring to pay off potential invaders or recruit mercenaries to repel barbarian incursions. The most controversial of Gibbon's assertions about this cultural change among Rome's elites was that Christianity contributed to it.

Gibbon himself had a curious religious history. While a student at Oxford in 1753, he converted to Catholicism. Anxious that this would cut him off from social advancement in Protestant Britain, Gibbon's father forced him to go and live in Lausanne, Switzerland, where, under a Calvinist pastor's supervision, he returned to Protestantism in 1754. Gibbon seems thereafter to have suspended his inquiries into religious truth.

In *Decline and Fall*, Gibbon did not disguise his conviction that the Christian religion had contributed mightily to Rome's political debilitation. In the first place, he argued, the Church effectively became a state within a state, an arrangement that no political entity can long tolerate without seriously compromising its authority. At the same time, Christianity diverted resources from Rome's military and infrastructure to churches, monasteries, and other religious institutions.

Another detriment of Christianity was what Gibbon believed to be its encouragement of pacifism. The Church's promise that faith in Christ opened the prospect of eternal life, he maintained, discouraged concern for worldly affairs and undermined believers' willingness to fight invaders.

Lastly, Gibbon maintained that Christianity sidetracked "the attention of the emperors [...] from camps to synods." [1] As more and more Romans became distracted by intra-Christian doctrinal disputes, they paid less attention to the empire's political well-being. The sheer fractiousness of these Christian quarrels contrasted with what Gibbon regarded as the far more tolerant, easygoing pagan cults.

Gibbon conceded that Christianity made the empire's fall less traumatic than it might have been. The new religion, he wrote, "broke the violence of the fall, and mollified the ferocious temper of the conquerors." [2] He likewise commended the Church's work with the poor and its stigmatizing of practices like gladiatorial matches, while praising certain Christian figures, such as Pope Gregory the Great, whose Roman patriotism injected new life into the city. Overall, however, Gibbon believed that Christianity ushered in "a servile and effeminate age." [3]

Since Gibbon's time, his assessment of religion's role in the Roman Empire has been subjected to considerable criticism. Pagan Romans may have had relatively relaxed views about religion. They were not, however, averse to sporadically persecuting Christians. As for the Jews, Pontius Pilate wasn't the first Roman official to go out of his way to offend their religious sensibilities. In AD 26 he attempted to bring ensigns of the emperor into Jerusalem. Fourteen years later, an increasingly erratic Emperor Gaius Caligula planned to install an enormous statue of himself in the Temple in Jerusalem, partly because he wanted to teach the Jews a lesson after the outbreak of violence between Greeks and Jews in Alexandria.[4] He was prevented from doing so only by his assassination in AD 41.

However we judge Gibbon's argument, we should not underrate *Decline and Fall*'s effect upon educated Europeans as its successive volumes were published over a thirteen-year period. For these were the years of the late Enlightenment, when criticisms of Christianity by many of the self-styled men of reason became sharper and bolder. *Decline and Fall* confirmed their belief that Christianity represented regression.

Christianity wasn't the only religion to receive an unfavorable review from Gibbon. He had equally unflattering things to say about Judaism.

In the midst of an ancient world characterized by tolerance of everyone else's superstitions, Gibbon wrote, a "single people refused

to join in the common intercourse of mankind."⁵ The Jews stood out
for their "sullen obstinacy" concerning their religious rites, "unsocial
manners," and "implacable hatred" of non-Jews. The "moderation of
the conquerors" was "insufficient to appease the [Jews'] jealous prej-
udices" as their land was reduced to a Roman province.⁶

Gibbon also insisted that the Jews were impervious to reason:
"[I]n contradiction to every known principle of the human mind,"
he asserted, "that singular people seems to have yielded a stronger
and more ready assent to the traditions of their remote ancestors than
to the evidence of their own senses."⁷

What should we make of Gibbon's criticism of the Jews and
their place in the Roman world? It's true that the Romans generally ruled conquered nations with a light hand, often preferring to work through client rulers such as Judaea's own King
Herod I. The Romans were exceptionally able at co-opting local
elites—especially by allowing them to acquire Roman citizen-
ship—so that they developed an interest in maintaining Roman
rule. Rabbi Saul of Tarsus, better known as the apostle Paul, wasn't
shy about invoking his status as a Roman citizen by birth when
he deemed it necessary (Acts 16:37; 22:22–30).

But as the Jews discovered, Rome's imperial authorities were not
the ancient world's equivalent of eighteenth-century *philosophes*.
Significant defiance of Rome usually resulted in brutal suppression
by the legions. When the Jewish Great Revolt erupted in AD 66, the
Romans waged seven years of ruthless warfare to crush Jewish resistance. The struggle ended only with the destruction of Jerusalem,
the Temple, and finally the fortress of Masada. And Rome's repres-
sion of the Bar-Kokhba Jewish Revolt of AD 132–136 was, if anything, even more thoroughgoing.

Equally questionable is Gibbon's portrait of the Jews as a people
closed to reason. For the Jews have a strong claim to being the first

people to articulate the world's comprehensibility to the human mind and to develop a robust conception of human freedom—intellectual conclusions that point to the reasonableness of belief in a rational Creator.

The miracle of the Jews

On several occasions, Gibbon mentions the Jews' violent antipathy to the idolatry that permeated the world surrounding them. Yet he never seems to have asked himself *why* many Jews would die rather than pay homage to the Canaanite Ba'al cults or the gods of Greece and Rome.

Obviously this stubbornness owed something to the Jews' belief that the one God, Yahweh, had commanded them not to worship other gods. The Hebrew scriptures repeatedly emphasize that the divine law has been decreed by a divine sovereign whom the sovereign's servants, Israel, must obey. The book of Deuteronomy's last ten chapters, for example, remind the Israelites that they are required to worship the one true God, warning that the worship of false gods will have terrible consequences.

The Jews' hostility to idolatry, however, also reflected their radically different conception of God and his relation to the material world, a conception that the philosopher and theologian Claude Tresmontant explored in the 1950s and 1960s. He pointed out that because of their understanding of a transcendent Creator, the Jews recognized that the entities worshipped by the Egyptians, Babylonians, Greeks, and Romans were not what they proclaimed them to be. Idols, the Jews insisted, had no real existence. To ascribe divinity to physical elements such as water, emotions such as envy, or practices such as war was literally non-sense for the Jews.

For the same reason, the Israelites considered it ridiculous to regard rulers, alive or dead, as gods. Man, they believed, had been created by a demanding but loving and good God in his *image*. Tresmontant stresses the contrast with those Near Eastern mythologies that presented man as the result of "a process in which wicked deeds mingled with acts of generation." [8]

The Jews also believed that the material world was not evil or beset by demonic contests. "The physical universe," writes Tresmontant, "is the first thing to be created, and God declares that it is very beautiful and very good." [9] This universe is presented in the Hebrew scriptures as ultimately permeated with order—not chaos and incomprehensibility. Much of this universe was thus understandable by the human beings made by this God in his image and similarly suffused with his order.

This belief in a good and ordered world challenged the supposition of the surrounding religions that the material world itself is malevolent—a view that was not clearly rebutted by Greek philosophers such as Plato. The Hebrews insisted that this material world was made for man and that its goodness would unfold under his cultivation.

This Jewish emphasis on the order built into a created world of which man is the apex had two critical consequences. First, Judaism's audacious confrontation of idolatry and pagan mythology was a powerful affirmation of man's *rationality*. Tresmontant explains:

> Here we have an intellectual revolution, a liberation, an act of free thought, a rejection of myth, and an effort to use reason, undoubtedly the most important that the human race has known in all its history. When the prophets of Israel bitterly rebuke pagan idolatry, they are doing something strictly *rational*. When they

refuse to sacrifice human children to idols or to myths, they carry their work of the use of reason into practical human conduct.... The inspiration which has led to this intellectual revolution ... is not something dictated from without on a servile human instrument. It is a revolution that works from within, and which starts to create a new, holy, reasonable humanity....[10]

The Jews' liberation of human reason from mythology and nature-worship amounted to one of humanity's most powerful "enlightenments." The Hebrew prophets were not philosophers as the Greeks understood this term, yet they played a major role in opening the human mind to objective reality. Several centuries later, Paul would tell Greeks and Romans that idolatry was a sign of ignorance and stupidity because a god made by human hands could be no god at all.

But what is especially important is the timing of these Jewish insights. As the legal philosopher John Finnis points out, "the Jewish people's accomplishment" of "reaching their settled and superior understanding of the universe's origins and natural intelligibility" occurred "centuries earlier than the Greeks reached their own standard and inferior understanding."[11]

The second important consequence of Judaism's understanding of the created universe was its accent on human *freedom*. In the Hebrew scriptures, human mistakes and errors are not caused by capricious Greek and Roman deities manipulating men. Nor did Judaism see human events as determined by fate, which characterized the pagan religions. In Greek lore, every man's destiny was the result of a thread spun, measured, and cut by the three Fates—Atropos, Clotho, and Lachesis—who themselves (revealingly) were daughters of the god of darkness, Erebus, and the goddess of night, Nyx.

The Hebrew Bible provides an entirely different account of human events. "The doctrine of freedom," Tresmontant writes, "is taught throughout the Old Testament. We always find that the God of Israel respects the created freedom which he appeals to, anxiously and earnestly, but which he never forces."[12] Genesis, for instance, does not portray God as inflicting the Fall upon man. Adam and Eve are banished from paradise because they freely chose to disobey God.

This theme of free will is summarized in the book of Ecclesiasticus, written by the Jewish scribe Ben Sira of Jerusalem sometime in the second century BC: "Do not say, 'Because of the Lord I left the right way'; for he will not do what he hates. Do not say, 'It was he who led me astray'; for he has no need of a sinful man" (15:11–12).

The same author follows this rebuff of fatalism with a strong affirmation of the reality of free will and free choice: "It was he who created man in the beginning, and he left him in the power of his own inclination. If you will, you can keep the commandments, and to act faithfully is a matter of your own choice. He has placed before you fire and water: stretch out your hand for whichever you wish. Before a man are life and death, and whichever he chooses will be given to him" (15:14–17). These words underline that, in many cases, it really is human beings' free choices that determine what is done—and nothing else.

But what about the Greeks?

At this juncture, some may interject: Surely the rise of reason and an attachment to liberty are primarily Greek achievements. Didn't the Hebrews and most other nations succumb to the rule of one Eastern empire after another? Wasn't it the Greeks who kept alive the cause of freedom when Persian despotism forced its way across the Bosporus twice in the fifth century BC?

It's worth considering what the consequences for the West might have been if Persian war banners had come to hang permanently on the Acropolis. But beyond counterfactual history, it would be reckless and ahistorical to discount the Greeks' immense contributions to Western philosophical, constitutional, political, legal, economic, and scientific thinking. It's hard to imagine the West as we know it today without Platonic metaphysics, the Socratic method, Thucydides's approach to history, Heraclitus's physics, or Aristotelian ethics.

It is likewise impossible, as no less an authority than Werner Heisenberg stated several times, to deny that the natural sciences' philosophical origins go back to Plato and beyond.[13] For Plato, the world's orderliness reflected a rational and mathematical structure that itself proceeded from an Intellect and was susceptible to human reason.

At this point, the word *logos* becomes important for the West. By Plato's time, it had become one of the Greek language's most common terms. The deepest meaning of *logos*—derived from the Greek verb "to speak"—was, according to the philologist Thorleif Boman, "the meaning, the ordered and reasonable content." It was also associated with "the reasonable man." [14]

For those philosophers called Stoics, *logos* was a way of explaining how human reason participated in a united and divine order in which God and the world were essentially the same in an almost pantheistic way. Stoics also used the term to describe the spirit or energy that animated all things.

This isn't quite the same idea as the Jewish understanding of God as the Creator. That said, Plato used *logos* to describe that which made it possible for human beings to understand themselves and their world.[15] The implication was that there was something self-conscious and rational at the beginning of time and of all things—including human reason. The importance of these references to human reason's extra-human origins can hardly be overestimated, but certain ideas in circulation made it difficult for the Greeks to realize the full potential of this insight—for example, the Greek understanding of choice. Aristotle spoke about choice, but he lacked a conception of *free* choice.[16] That makes all the difference in the world for what we understand to be freedom's nature.

Another major obstacle was the influence of those Greek thinkers who strongly doubted human reason's capacity to know much at all. The so-called "Skeptics," such as Pyrrho of Elis, denied the mind's capacity to understand anything important with certainty. He and like-minded philosophers believed that our senses are essentially deceitful. Human minds, they argued, hardly penetrate beyond the appearance of things.[17]

Such viewpoints were not marginal to Greek intellectual life. For long periods, Skeptics dominated what had been Plato's Academy in Athens.[18] Their teaching was reinforced by philosophers such as Epicurus, who maintained that the universe was made up of nothing but an infinite number of material particles.[19] For "Epicureans," if there were gods (about which they were doubtful), they were a far-removed, self-obsessed elite who had nothing to do with everyday human life.

Other Greek philosophers sought to produce accounts for human existence that essentially dispensed with anything like Plato's Intellect. Known as "the Mocker" for his willingness to scoff at those he considered delusional, Democritus, possibly a contemporary of Socrates, tried to understand the world without any reference to an uncaused First Cause. He offered a mechanistic account: that everything that happens is a consequence of atoms moving, touching, and interacting.[20] There can be no non-material directive cause of the type identified by Plato. Instead, all proceeds from chance and, ultimately, from nothing: "In the beginning was the Void."

But the most serious impediment to the Greeks' appreciation of reason was their religion. In the ancient pagan world, "religion" did not mean a set of beliefs about the divine that were somewhat removed from culture, politics, and economic life. For pagans, religion was primarily about the beliefs and practices that bound together entire societies, including their political and cultural dimensions, while also linking men to their ancestors and the divinities.[21] Temples integrated the human and divine realms. The gods were everywhere and permeated everything.

This binding character was given particular expression through public cultic activities (festivals, sacrifices, oracles, and so on). Everyone was expected to participate in these rites as a matter of piety and to placate the temperamental and egotistic gods lest they lash out at the community. But religious observance was also a demonstration of loyalty to the *polis*. That is why Jews and Christians, who were unwilling to participate in the state-supervised religious cults, were suspected by Greeks and Romans of being atheists and potential subversives.

Religion in this sense was pervasive in the Greek and Roman world. It was consequently difficult for most people to escape the conviction that the human world was ultimately at the mercy of some often unpleasant and very fickle deities. That conviction in turn gave rise to an enormous intellectual problem. Put simply, how could a universe of selfish, irrational deities be reconciled with Aristotle's assertion that by studying physical phenomena man could discern the laws of nature, let alone with Archimedes's mathematics or Hipparchus's astronomy and geometry?

Athens meets Jerusalem

One by-product of this conundrum was the gradual emergence of carefully worded criticisms of Greek religion. These can be found in

Socrates and Aristotle.[22] The latter even ventured to claim that many mythologies served some all too human purposes.[23]

Unlike the Skeptics, these Greeks were looking for an account of the divine that could be reconciled with human rationality. Aristotle eventually concluded that "God is a living being, eternal, most good; and therefore life and a continuous eternal existence belong to God; for that is what God is."[24] "Eternal" encompasses not only the future but also the past and present. This leads us to Aristotle's idea of First Cause: that there must be one great unmoved and unchanging Mover, eternal and necessary, who has always existed and who continues holding everything in place.[25] That meant it was impossible to believe that the world came into being by accident.

This is inching closer to Jewish conceptions of the Creator. In fact, by this stage, the Greek world knew a great deal about Judaism. Jews had been living outside the boundaries of the ancient kingdoms of Israel and Judah for more than six centuries before Christ. Large diaspora communities were found from Babylon to Rome.[26] One twentieth-century historian of the Jewish people, Salo W. Baron, estimates that by the middle of the first century AD, there were approximately eight million Jews in the world, of whom between five and six million lived outside modern Israel.[27]

The exposure of Greek to Jew was facilitated by the translation of the Hebrew scriptures into Greek at Alexandria, an important crossroads of culture and learning, between 287 and 130 BC. One reason for the production of what is known as the Septuagint was that many diaspora Jews were losing the ability to speak and read Hebrew. The explication of the scriptures in Greek to diaspora congregations fueled a desire for a Greek translation of the scriptures.

The translation of the Septuagint had two important side effects. First, Jewish translators had to consider how to express Hebrew ideas in terms understandable to Greek speakers. Second, Greeks could now study Jewish thought, including its conception of God and the universe.

While many Greeks were fascinated by the mystery cults that proliferated in the East, Judaism presented Greeks with something different: a bond between human rationality and the revelation of a particular God—a God who was demanding and often inscrutable but who rescued his people from their mistakes and, compared with pagan deities, was reasonable, just, and moral.

This Greek encounter with Jewish thought accounts in part for the emergence of those called "God-fearers," non-Jews attracted to Judaism, especially its monotheism, clear theological beliefs, and precise expectations for behavior. The contrast with the muddle of the pagan cults was stark. The more perceptive God-fearers surely took sustenance from those scriptural verses (e.g., Psalms 2:7–9, 47:8–9, and 72:8) promising that Israel's God would be not only the God of the Hebrews but the Lord of all nations. God-fearers loosely attached themselves to synagogues and adopted Judaism's moral precepts, but they remained somewhat outside the Jewish world, disregarding particular parts of the Mosaic law, like the dietary restrictions.[28]

The Greco-Jewish encounter was not a one-way process. Hellenic ideas appear to have had little influence in Judaea and Galilee, but educated diaspora Jews like Saul of Tarsus, himself trained in the Jerusalem school of Rabban Gamaliel I, one of the great Pharisaic doctors of the law, were conversant with Greek thought and life.[29] They knew Greek philosophical terminology, the difference between Epicureans and Stoics, the names of Greek and Roman gods, and the beliefs of the pagan religions. In a multiethnic commercial town like Tarsus in modern-day southeast Turkey, with its active academy and enormous library, an intellectually and linguistically gifted Jew like Saul couldn't help but swim in Greek ideas and culture.

Figures like the Jewish scholar Philo of Alexandria (25 BC–AD 50) moved comfortably between the Hellenic and Jewish worlds. A member of a priestly family, Philo was also a Roman citizen and deeply involved in Roman politics. His brothers and nephews served as Roman officials. But Philo categorically understood himself to be a Jew and visited Jerusalem at least once.[30]

Throughout his writings, Philo employs Greek concepts to elucidate aspects of Jewish belief. The word *logos* signifies at least eleven ideas in Philo's reflections.[31] It is one of his ways to describe the Word of God, linking it to the Jewish understanding of a personal and rational Creator who remains active in his creation, giving it meaning and order. Philo also uses *logos* to explain how human reason reflects God's reason as the all-pervading divine *Logos*. This unique gift of God, Philo writes, enables men to "comprehend the nature of all bodies and of all things" and, unlike other created life forms, to enjoy the power of free volition.[32]

Philo's effort to bridge the Jewish and Greek worlds was aided by a Hebrew concept that in certain ways paralleled *logos*. The Hebrew word *dabhar* joined the notion of "dynamic deed" and the concept of "word." *Dabhar*'s most basic meaning was "dynamism," or what drives forward from behind.[33] But the Israelites also used *dabhar* to describe how Yahweh made his essence recognizable to human beings, an essence that always had moral and spiritual content. This is one reason the Decalogue is called "the ten words" (Exodus 34:28). Hence the *dabhar* of Yahweh, Boman stresses, is "never a force of nature." Rather, it is "always the function of a conscious and moral personality."[34]

This distinguished Yahweh from the gods of other Middle Eastern peoples, whose deities were personified forces of nature.[35] By contrast, *dabhar* was the act not of many beings but of one mind. Boman finds in *dabhar* something resembling "the Greek *logos* idea."[36]

The correspondences between *dabhar* and *logos* are thus clear. The former stresses dynamism more than the latter. But we can see why someone like Philo regarded *logos* as a way of conveying some of the associations of *dabhar* to diaspora Jews.

The Christian revolution

Given the interpenetration of Greek and Jewish thought, we need to ask: What kept those Greeks and Romans, increasingly convinced of the pagan religions' irrationality, from embracing Judaism?

While there is evidence of a sizable number of converts to Judaism (called "proselytes" by the Jews) throughout the Roman Empire by the first century AD, there were considerable deterrents to conversion, such as the Jewish revolts against Roman rule, which made many doubt that Jews could be loyal to the emperor. [37]

These suspicions were magnified by the Jews' exemption from military service and, most importantly, from participation in the imperial state cult, from the reign of Augustus onward, of Caesar as the *divi filius* (son of the divine one). Even the bargain struck between the Jews and Rome for the sake of civil peace—that Jews would pray *to* Yahweh *for* Rome and the emperor—did not dispel the sense that Jews were insufficiently patriotic.

Then there was the fact that while the imperial authorities granted various concessions to Jews, Romans and Greeks didn't particularly like Jews. For many Romans and Greeks, Jews were another species of barbarian because they weren't Roman or Greek. [38] And, as always, Jewish economic success aroused antipathy. [39]

Another deterrent was that, while Judaism proclaimed a universal God who had worked wonders inside and outside Israel and thus exercised authority in all places and times, this same God was bound by a special link to a particular nation. Jewish rituals and worship were closely connected to specifically Jewish historical events and locations, such as the Temple in Jerusalem, which were largely closed to non-Jews.

Certainly Jews interacted daily with Greeks and Romans. Even those who were strictly observant didn't live in isolation from pagans. Jews argued among themselves not about *whether* but about *how much* they could engage with non-Jews. Nonetheless, they retained a deep sense of "us" and "them." Even as Hellenized a Jew as Philo appreciated the huge gulf between him and the non-Jew.

It was Christianity that upended this apparently intractable situation—forever.

From the beginning, Christianity taught that being born a non-Jew was no longer an impediment to a full relationship with the God of Abraham, Isaac, and Jacob. The universal mission of the Christian church was reflected in its dispensing with most of the rituals and prohibitions of the Mosaic law but without contradicting the revelation given to the Jews. Instead, Christianity imparted the essence of this message in its fullness to all men. The Christian religion maintained the Hebrews' understanding of God as Creator, of man as a created being with reason and free will, and of the material world as subordinate to man, who would no longer worship creatures as gods. It also underscored the Decalogue as *the* core moral code for *all* peoples.

Christianity did not engage in mythologizing. Just as Judaism proclaimed that God actually spoke to a real man named Abraham, the writers of the Christian Gospels insisted that they were relating eyewitness accounts of real events.

Christ's Resurrection, for instance, was not presented or understood as a comforting fable based on the projection of a small community's feelings after its gentle leader's brutal execution by Roman authorities. The Resurrection was depicted as having taken place at a specific moment in history at a particular place and having been verified by eyewitnesses. The Christian church's earliest councils defended the *realism* of this account against any inclination to mythologize it.

The parts of the Greco-Roman world that were disillusioned with mythology and sympathetic to key Jewish beliefs proved receptive to the Christian message. The new religion affirmed many propositions that some Greeks and Romans already viewed as reasonable or dimly grasped but could not extricate from the chaos of pagan religion.

Christianity, however, stressed three ideas that were particularly influential in the development of Western culture. The first of these was God's rational and creative nature, a theme that is powerfully expressed in the opening words of the Gospel of John. The evangelist took the first verse of the book of Genesis, "In the beginning, God created the heavens and the earth," and adapted it to "In the beginning was the Word"—in Greek, "In the beginning was the *Logos*." As if to stress this point, the first words about love contained in the First Epistle of John (2:5)—generally considered to be by the same author as the fourth Gospel—occur *after* the statement that "God is light" (1:5), referring to the truth, intellect, and intelligibility of God. To Greek, Roman, and diaspora Jewish readers familiar with the language of *logos*, these words made the point that the Christian God is not irrational. On the contrary, Christ is reason incarnate.

At the same time, many readers of John's Gospel, especially Hellenized Jews, would have understood "the Word" as "the Word-as-reason," embracing features of *dabhar*: moral agency, self-consciousness, dynamism, and creativity. This *Logos* wasn't an abstract metaphysical postulate. Jesus was the *Logos* made flesh: the reasonable God who stood at the beginning of time and who had entered directly into human history. This God's innate reasonableness also meant that his love could never be corrupted into sentimentality.

The second point stressed by Christianity was the affirmation that all people are capable of knowing the truth through natural reason. Pagans noticed the Christian stress on truth's knowability. In the dialogue *Octavius* (ca. AD 200), recorded by the Christian apologist Marcus Minucius Felix, a pagan mockingly refers to Christians as "the high priests of truth" as he defends uncertainty, relativism, and probability.[40]

Christianity's relentless insistence that human beings can know Truth with a capital "T" extended to moral truth. Paul insisted that the core meaning of the Decalogue given by Moses to the Jews and rigorously reaffirmed by Christ (Matthew 19:16–22) was the very same moral law that God had written on every person's heart (Romans 2:13–15).

"Heart," for Paul, meant the natural knowledge of moral good and moral evil inscribed into human reason itself. Paul was clearly referring to the idea of natural law—a way of thought that had been developed by Stoic and Aristotelian philosophers. By suggesting that there is something essentially unchanging about human nature and the human mind, Paul was proposing more than just another ethical theory. He was daring to say that all people could know basic truths about right, wrong, good, and evil through reason and that people could choose to live good lives even in the deeply imperfect non-Jewish cultures of his time.

This doesn't mean that Paul believed pagans could be content to be virtuous idol-worshipers. While Greek philosophy had achieved some important insights, they did not, in Paul's view, encompass the whole truth. Even more basically, Paul regarded the Greek and Roman public cults as abominations.

Paul's words nevertheless amounted to a radical affirmation of the equality of everyone—not just those males who were full citizens, but also resident aliens, women, children, and slaves. All were fully human and bore concrete responsibilities in the face of objective morality. This equality not only appealed to those who were used and abused by the powerful in the pagan world but also supported Paul's emphasis upon a new way of living—the doing of good deeds grounded in truth—which followed from *faith* in the God-Man who was the Word-*Logos* and from doing what human *reason* recognized as good and true.

Right choice and action thus reflected this seamless integration of faith and reason, which led Christianity to embrace Judaism's strict sexual ethic. Christians were not pursuing rules for the sake of rules or even social order. As the Anglican New Testament scholar N. T. Wright observes, Christians saw sexual impropriety as a sure sign that one did not know God and was heedless of his call to freely choose the good.[41]

That people can choose and act rightly implies that they can also choose and act wrongly. The third idea that Christianity stressed, then, is *freedom*.

Christ's famous admonition to give to Caesar what belongs to Caesar and to God what belongs to God (Mark 12:17) is widely regarded as radicalizing the Jewish conviction that the power of earthly rulers is limited by God's divine law, a conviction that would become a crucial feature of the Western understanding of government power.

Even more importantly, Christ acknowledged on several occasions that people were free to follow him or not. This freedom is consistent with the Jewish affirmation of free will in the face of good and evil, but it also implies limits on the ability of others—including the state—to tell people what to do.

There was, however, something else that Christianity stressed about freedom, namely, freedom is more than an absence of constraint. Man is free *for* something.

That something is excellence—the excellence that is the fruit of using our reason to understand the world and unfold its potential *and* the excellence of freely choosing what reason and revelation show us to be true. This is what Paul meant when he wrote, "For you were called to freedom, brethren; only do not use your freedom as an opportunity for the flesh, but through love be servants of one another" (Galatians 5:13–14). Paul means more than not using one's liberty to resist the pagan world's dehumanizing temptations. That is important but merely a preamble to a higher freedom, which is found in living good lives as individuals and communities.

Nineteen hundred years later, the Polish-born American rabbi Abraham Heschel made a similar point. The culmination of the people of Israel's liberation from slavery in Egypt, he argued, was their reception of the Decalogue. The first commandment reminded the Hebrews that it was God who freed them from oppression. But the last commandment, which condemns envy, exhorted Jews to conquer *themselves* by freeing themselves from base instincts and achieving "inner liberty." [42]

Into the West's DNA

When we consider these three Christian teachings—God's rational nature, a natural law that all men can discern, and human freedom as the power to choose the good and the true—we start to understand Christianity's great interior power. This religion combined universalism with a respect for people's reason and freedom and a call to change themselves and their world for the better.

Such a faith would have been attractive to many Greeks and Romans, who were immensely proud of their intellectual and cultural accomplishments. In Christianity, they found a faith that respected many of their successes but also reconciled them with the idea of a rational Creator in ways that paganism never could.

Christianity's integration of what might be called the Greek Enlightenment into Judaism's unique religious achievement set the pagan religions that had blurred the horizons of the Greco-Roman world on the path to extinction. The inconsistency between the Greek and Roman myths and the knowledge achieved by reason led to the myths being replaced by belief in a reasonable Deity. Men saw that religion should be concerned with the truth about reality and therefore ought to be compatible with reason. The result was a civilizational platform that the Greek and Roman philosophers could not have constructed on their own.

We should not imagine that paganism's replacement by Christianity went uncontested. Paul's use of recognizably Stoic language in his encounter with leading Greek minds in the Areopagus in Athens, the honored home of philosophy, did not convince all his listeners (Acts 17:16–34). As soon as Paul referred to Christ's resurrection, many laughed at him. Others politely dismissed him, though some, it is recorded, were persuaded.

Almost four hundred years later, one of Christianity's greatest thinkers, Augustine of Hippo, was asked by a certain Marcellus to combat the many pagan philosophers who maintained that the abandonment of the old Roman and Greek religions had paved the way for the sack of Rome by the Visigoths in AD 410. Augustine's response to this accusation resulted in one of the West's most important books, *The City of God*. Such intellectual struggles were further complicated by disputes with the many Jews who did not embrace Christianity, not to mention furious doctrinal debates among Christians.

Christianity continued to spread, however, and its approach to faith and reason became embedded in the West's self-understanding. As early as the second century, Christianity's first philosophers were unpacking the meaning of Paul's references to natural law as universal principles that apply to all peoples and give meaning to their liberty.[43]

One of the best known of these philosophers, Justin Martyr, stressed the Christian faith's reasonableness. Christians, he declared, were the true followers of the *Logos*. Justin's *First Apology* repeatedly highlighted the irrationality of pagan beliefs, drew parallels between Christianity and Platonic thought, and emphasized that the Hebrew prophets had articulated a more cogent explanation of the universe's origins than the Greeks.[44] Justin thus joined biblical monotheism with the Greek search for the ultimate foundations of reality.[45]

Other Christians, such as the Greek theologian Clement of Alexandria (ca. AD 150–ca. AD 215), described Christianity as "the true philosophy" and emphasized the active presence of the divine *Logos* throughout history, eventually incarnated in Christ.[46] They relied on Greek concepts to explain theological ideas while correcting certain aspects of Platonic and Stoic thought, assisting the Greek mind's great escape from the incubus of pagan mythology.[47]

Despite the turmoil inside and outside the Church as the Western Roman Empire collapsed, the project of integrating faith and reason continued down the centuries, reaching its apex in the thought of the thirteenth-century theologian Thomas Aquinas. He engaged in a thoroughgoing study of Aristotelian philosophy, evaluating it in light of the scriptures and the thought of figures such as Augustine and applying his conclusions to subjects ranging from metaphysics and the natural sciences to politics and law.

In no other culture was this integration of faith and reason achieved as systematically or for such a sustained period. Between the eighth and tenth centuries, during the Umayyad and Abbasid caliphates, for instance, the Islamic school of theology known as the Mu'tazilites developed a sophisticated theory about the relation between reason and revelation, according a high place to human rationality and acknowledging some degree of free will.[48] The Mu'tazilites, however, never attained an ascendancy in Islam. They were eventually marginalized and were regarded as heretical before disappearing.[49]

In the West, the integration of reason and faith acquired a name, Scholasticism, and was strongly attached to what is called deductive reasoning—proceeding from general premises to a specific conclusion, as in Aristotle's famous formulation: All men are mortal; Socrates is a man; therefore Socrates is mortal.

The premises of this argument (all men are mortal; Socrates is a man) are not empirical. They are *self-evident*. Deductive reasoning follows the *logic* of a chain of concepts. You find it expressed, for example, in Aquinas's five arguments for God's existence.[50]

The institution that seeks the truth

The spread of this method of reasoning owed much to the emergence in medieval Europe of one institution in particular. Usually linked to a cathedral or monastery, the *universitas magistrorum et scholarium* was designed to educate clergymen in the Western Church's universal language (Latin) and subjects like theology, philosophy, logic, rhetoric, and geometry. These were the intellectual tools required by those destined for important ecclesiastical and civil office.

Something else, however, also drove the establishment of these institutions. Few have explained this better than Benedict XVI did in a speech to French intellectuals in Paris on September 12, 2008, exactly two years after his Regensburg address and seven years and one day after the 2001 terrorist attacks.[51] The date of this speech was no less significant than the location: the Collège des Bernardins, founded in 1248 by the abbot of Clairvaux, Stephen of Lexington. It served as a residence for Cistercian monks studying at the University of Paris until the French Revolution.

Why, Benedict asked, had monks come to study at places like the Collège des Bernardins? They did not regard themselves as in the "culture-building" business. They were there to search for God (*quaerere Deum*)—for the fullness of Truth—with the resources at their disposal. One of these resources was the Word of God, the Hebrew and Christian scriptures. The monks studied these texts so they could explain and defend what they believed to be the truths of Christianity. In Benedict's words: "The classic formulation of the Christian faith's intrinsic need to make itself communicable to others is a phrase from the First Letter of Peter, which in medieval theology was regarded as the biblical basis for the work of theologians: 'Always have your answer ready for people who ask you the reason (the *logos*) for the hope that you all have' (3:15). The *Logos*, the reason for hope must become *apo-logía*; it must become a response."

In the same address, the pope explained that the monks recognized that the truth about ultimate realities revealed in the Bible was also attainable through reason. Belief that there is a God who is intrinsically rational, he told his highly secular audience, is itself reasonable: "[T]he deepest layer of human thinking and feeling somehow knows that [God] must exist, that at the beginning of all things, there must be not irrationality, but creative Reason—not blind chance, but freedom."

Human reason itself, Benedict was arguing, *knows* that man's capacity for reason cannot arise from irrationality. Our very nature thus testifies to a divine Creator, as does the order which our minds see in creation. As Paul proclaimed, "Ever since the creation of the world, his invisible nature, namely, his eternal power and deity, has been clearly perceived in the things that have been made" (Romans 1:20).

As important as Benedict's reaffirmation of Christianity's unique integration of faith and reason was the setting in which he did so: one of the church institutions that gave rise to the university, which attained its decisive form *in* the West. This is why the pope concluded his speech by insisting that this "search for God and the readiness to listen to him" are what "gave Europe's culture its foundation."

We thus see how Christianity's concern for reason and faith fostered institutions that produced a renaissance of inquiry not only into theology but also into a multitude of other disciplines. It is simply untrue, for example, that the Middle Ages marked a hiatus in the progress of the natural sciences in the West. In the thirteenth century, theologians such as Albertus Magnus underscored the importance of observation, experimentation, and what we call "data." Franciscan friars like Roger Bacon (ca. 1212–1292) made astronomical calculations that eventually led to the reform of the calendar. Bacon was especially noted for reiterating Aristotle's point that facts need to be collected and studied before statements on scientific matters can be made.[52] The fourteenth-century bishop Nicolas Oresme of Lisieux wrote extensively on geometry and astronomy, made important discoveries in the realm of dynamics and velocity, helped develop the notion of fractional powers in mathematics, and enhanced understanding of the functions of money.[53]

Throughout this same period, Jewish scholars living in the West made their own contributions to the natural sciences. Levi ben Gershon (1288–1344) was a mathematician of such stature that Catholic bishops would consult him about mathematical problems. He also was the first premodern astronomer to estimate stellar distances correctly.[54] Another Jewish mathematician and astronomer, Immanuel ben Jacob Bonfils (ca. 1300–1377), wrote a manuscript on eclipses. His astronomical tables, which forecast lunar and solar positions, were used by sailors until the mid-1600s.[55]

The Europeans who achieved these scientific advances made use of knowledge from the East, which began to reach the West in the tenth century. The Muslim Arab Ibn al-Haytham (965–1040), for example, who developed the science of optics, was part of a flourishing of science, mathematics, and natural philosophy throughout the Arab and Persian worlds. Today we also have a better sense of the enormous amount of Greek learning that was preserved and developed in the Byzantine Empire and among Middle Eastern Jews and Christians and later translated into Arabic.[56] These Eastern scholars never lost intellectual contact with Western Europe and consequently transmitted to the West much of the knowledge that they had conserved and advanced.[57]

Many medieval scholars pursued disciplines such as astronomy because they needed to calculate, for example, the correct date of Easter. In other instances, Christian teachings such as caring for the sick led monks to deepen their understanding of medicine. Even the process of discerning whether a miracle had occurred moved some churchmen to understand the natural world more deeply.

Medieval men were more interested in the *results* of their experiments and observations than in scientific theories, and the division between philosophy and the physical sciences was less precise than it would subsequently become.[58] But the foundation of all these inquiries was an understanding that the world is characterized by order, that the human mind can comprehend it, and that because the world is the work of God, it merits study.[59]

But what happens if that foundation breaks down?

This was precisely Benedict's warning to the West in the final paragraph of his Paris speech: "A purely positivistic culture which tried to drive the question concerning God into the subjective realm, as being unscientific, would be the capitulation of reason, the renunciation of its highest possibilities, and hence a disaster for humanity, with very grave consequences." [60]

Benedict asserted that once reason ceases to regard knowledge of God as part of the search for truth, then reason, far from being liberated, is unduly constricted—not least because it is closed off from its ultimate source. And that, in Benedict's view, is a betrayal of the very heart of Western culture.

It is an irony of history that the separation of reason from faith began during the same Middle Ages that witnessed Aquinas's triumph as the master integrator of reason and faith.

Faith versus reason

Aquinas's endeavors formed part of the same search for truth that the monks in the Collège des Bernardins pursued. But like Augustine, Aquinas's quest was also prompted by the need to respond to specific intellectual challenges.

Aquinas was particularly concerned about the tendency, usually found among various Franciscan orders, to reject Greek philosophy. Aquinas held that the knowledge imparted by faith surpassed that of reason, but he also believed that disengaging from Greek philosophy or embracing the wrong type of Greek thought would diminish the Church's capacity to respond to criticisms of the Christian faith.

A second group that worried Aquinas were the Averroists, a school of medieval philosophy influenced by the Muslim philosopher Ibn Rushd, known in Latin as Averroes. Many Averroists, Aquinas held, argued in favor of what amounted to a theory of "double truth." While truth was one, the truths knowable through revelation and faith were not only different but could contradict those truths attainable through philosophy and science. This contradiction was possible because, the argument went, an all-powerful God could will anything to be its opposite. Each part of the contradiction was thus true.[61]

This dichotomy perturbed Aquinas. He recognized that believing there could be contradictory truths necessarily undermined the idea that all truth is one, despite the protestations of the Averroists to the contrary. Furthermore, many might decide that reason and faith had little to do with each other. Not only would such conclusions undermine what had taken Greek, Jewish, and Christian thinkers centuries to achieve, but if revelation became the realm of faith-without-reason, then one could easily conclude that God himself wasn't rational. And if that were the case, some might start to believe that in the beginning was not the *Logos* but rather a Divine Will, a Being that could will one truth today, its opposite tomorrow, or even truth and untruth at the same time. The search for truth—not just religious and philosophical truth but also scientific truth—would be futile, and the door would be open to an *a priori* commitment to relativism.

It's tempting to regard such medieval debates as greatly removed from the practical problems facing today's Western societies. Unfortunately for the West, the separation of the world of reason from the world of faith would have grave consequences, many of which weigh heavily on us today.

CHAPTER THREE

Reason and Its Corruptions

*This most beautiful system of the sun, planets, and comets,
could only proceed from the counsel and dominion of an
intelligent and powerful Being.... This Being governs all
things, not as the soul of the world, but as Lord over all;
and on account of his dominion he is wont to be called
Lord God Pantokrator, or Universal Ruler.*
—Isaac Newton

I t's an understatement to say that the publication of Newton's *Philosophiae Naturalis Principia Mathematica* on July 5, 1687, was a pivotal event in history. In many ways, it proved decisive for the direction of the West. Nothing would ever be the same. Stating basic rules and hypotheses from which an astounding range of calculations and explanations could be developed, the *Principia* represented a revolution in the natural sciences. Nature's secrets, it seemed, had not only been unlocked but had become quantifiable.

Outlining Newton's law of universal gravitation and his laws of motion, the *Principia* established the basis of classical mechanics in physics. It was now possible to explain the acceleration of planets in their orbits that the mathematician and astronomer Johannes Kepler (1571–1630) had observed. These and other discoveries led to new technologies that would reshape the world. The awe in which Newton, the very embodiment of the Enlightenment, came to be held is reflected in Alexander Pope's rapturous couplet:

> Nature and nature's law lay hid in night:
> God said, Let Newton be! And all was light.[1]

Newton and countless Enlightenment thinkers constantly invoked "nature": natural religion, natural rights, state of nature, Nature's God, etc. But for them, nature did not mean simply the natural world. Nature was, like God, universal—it traversed time from the present and back to the creation of the world. Nature was also inside all human beings; it was what made each human being *human*. Finally, nature was a synonym for the Divinity: that which created all things and was the source of all moral principles.

There are parallels here with the way that pre-Enlightenment Western minds thought about the nature of God and human reason, parallels that become clearer when we recall that one reason Newton wrote the *Principia* was to refute what he regarded as the materialist assumptions underlying the theory of planetary movements proposed by the French philosopher René Descartes (1596–1650). The planets' consistent motion was not, Newton held, a matter of "mechanical causes" but the doing of the *Pantokrator*.

Pantokrator is a Greek word used in the Septuagint for Hebrew designations of God such as *El Shaddi* (God Almighty) and *Yahweh Sabaoth* (Lord of Hosts). It also appears in Paul's second letter to the Corinthians (2 Cor. 6:18) and the book of Revelation.[2] Other meanings of the word include "Ruler of All" and "Sustainer of the World."

Christ Pantokrator is one of the most common images in the Christian iconography of the East.

Newton's use of *Pantokrator* was therefore no accident. To Europe's educated classes, it signaled his disagreement not only with materialist explanations of the planets' motions but also with the rationales offered by some of those who were known as Deists.

Emerging in the late seventeenth century, Deism entailed a belief in God, but it was not a monolithic set of beliefs. Some Deists held that God was a great clockmaker who had created a self-sustaining world and did not intervene in the natural or human order. Others thought that this Deity remained involved in this world through the workings of Providence, understood as a spiritual power that directed human affairs toward good ends. Most Deists rejected the idea of any direct revelation of God beyond what men could discover through reason and the study of society and the natural world. They also denied miracles and viewed organized religion with a skeptical eye.[3]

For Newton, God was far more than a clockmaker. The freedom of human will, he maintained, mirrored God's creative power. The existence in man of free-willed self-motion was a living repudiation of materialist and atheist explanations for the universe. His God was a Creator who had called the world into being and was intimately involved with that same world all the time.

This conviction was grounded not only in philosophy and natural science. Newton's Creator was the God of the Jewish and Christian scriptures and the preexistent *Logos*, the rational force within the universe.[4]

In the most thorough study of Newton's religious thought, Rob Iliffe, a historian of science, illustrates that Newton's "deep Christian faith was the most important aspect of his life."[5] Impatient with those who mocked religion, Newton held that God had revealed in the scriptures much about himself and the world that man would not otherwise know. No less a philosopher than John Locke (1632–1704) remarked on Newton's profound knowledge of the scriptures. Newton studied these texts intensely but also immersed himself in early Church histories and the writings of Church Fathers such as Ignatius of Antioch. He was as impressed by the learning of the Hebrew prophets as he was with those Greek thinkers who had grappled with scientific subjects.[6]

This extensive reading led Newton to embrace some decidedly unorthodox views about central Christian dogmas like the Trinity. "He was," Iliffe states, "no libertine, deist or atheist, but, according to the doctrines of his own church, he was a heretic."[7] But his heterodoxies did not inhibit him from directly criticizing divine-clockmaker Deism in the essay "Scholium Generale," which he appended to the 1713 edition of the *Principia*. "A god without dominion, providence, and final causes," Newton wrote, "is nothing else but Fate and Nature." To emphasize his point, Newton added, "Blind metaphysical necessity could produce no variety of things. All that diversity of things...could only arise from nothing but the ideas and will of a Being necessarily existing."[8]

Despite this affirmation of a rational, active Creator by the hero of the Enlightenment, the relation between reason and faith became more ambiguous and even conflicted in the West from Newton's time onward. The great strides to come in the natural and social sciences would be accompanied by considerable regression in other fields, including the West's understanding of the breadth and depth of reason.

Faith as superstition

Though Deism was on the rise during Newton's lifetime, most men of science still shared his non-deistic understanding of God's nature. Kepler, for instance, was a deeply religious Lutheran who believed that the Creator's plan for his world was knowable through reason and revelation. Newton's compatriot, Robert Boyle, a chemist, inventor, physicist, philosopher, theologian, financier of missionary activities in India, and pious Anglican, wrote a book titled *The Christian Virtuoso, Shewing that by being addicted to Experimental Philosophy, a Man is rather Assisted, than Indisposed, to be a Good* Christian (1690).

Though none of these intellectuals saw a necessary conflict between religious faith and scientific reason, the Enlightenment is usually portrayed as a reaction against the wars of religion of the sixteenth and seventeenth centuries, the political power wielded by Christian churches, and the key religious claims of Judaism and Christianity.

There is much truth to this portrayal. Some Enlightenment thinkers were skeptical about certain Christian propositions, wondered about God's existence, and insisted that religion had impeded progress. In 1904, a leading French physicist and devout Catholic, Pierre Duhem, lamented that the Galileo affair had left many European thinkers disillusioned with Christianity.[9]

Over time, disillusion grew into outright hostility in some quarters. In a preface to Voltaire's epic poem *La Henriade*, the eighteenth century's symbol of enlightened absolutism, Frederick the Great of Prussia (1712–1786), insisted that "The more one is enlightened, the less one is superstitious."[10] By "superstitious," Frederick primarily meant Christian. In his *Political Testament* (1768), Frederick called the Christian faith "an old metaphysical fiction, stuffed with wonders, contradictions, and absurdities. It was spawned in the fevered imagination of the Orientals, and then spread to our Europe, where some fanatics espoused it, where some intriguers pretended to be convinced by it, and where some imbeciles actually believed it."[11]

Voltaire's sentiments on this subject mirrored those of his royal patron. In correspondence with Frederick, Voltaire complained, "Our [religion] is assuredly the most ridiculous, the most absurd, and the most bloody religion which has ever infected this world. Your Majesty will do the human race an eternal service by extirpating this infamous superstition."[12]

Contempt for Christianity during the Enlightenment was often accompanied by calls for religious toleration, in particular by Locke and the French Huguenot philosopher Pierre Bayle (1647–1706). In Frederick's predominately Protestant Prussia, toleration was extended to Catholics, even though the king considered Catholicism the most ludicrous of faiths.[13] This antipathy, which the philosopher-king never bothered to disguise, did not prevent him from building St. Hedwig's Cathedral in Berlin for his Catholic subjects.

Frederick's toleration was more limited when it came to Jews. Despite some liberalization around the edges, most Jews in Prussia continued living under restrictions not applied to other faiths. Apart from long-standing anti-Semitism, these policies may have reflected Voltaire's influence. He regularly mocked Jews for their alleged barbarism.[14]

As we have seen, anti-Jewish sentiments pervaded the writings of Voltaire's contemporary Edward Gibbon. One of Gibbon's criticisms of Judaism and Christianity involved the ways in which these religions had purportedly inhibited something of great concern to Enlightenment thinkers—progress.

The new science

Progress is one of the West's great motifs. While commonly associated with the Enlightenment, the idea of progress owes much to the book of Genesis's emphasis upon man's transforming the world through work, as well as to the more general biblical theme that God has a plan for the world which human beings are helping to realize.

The Jewish and Christian conception of time as linear gave the West a sense of moving from a beginning to an end. The book of Revelation (1:8) expresses this movement in God's declaration that "I am the Alpha and the Omega," using the first and last letters of the Greek alphabet to denote the beginning and end of time. This view of history as moving toward an end contrasted with the Stoic under-standing of history as cyclical, with everything, despite upheavals, conflagrations, and occasional restarts, being seen as simply part of an unending, repetitive churn.[15]

Gibbon's invocation of "progress" implied something different and more specific: the cultivation of *science*. "The histories of empires," he wrote, "is that of the miseries of mankind; the history of the sciences is that of their splendor and happiness."[16] The historian Hugh Trevor-Roper observes that for Gibbon, the sciences "meant useful science, experimental Baconian science, directed to the understanding of nature and the improvement of human life."[17] Enlightenment writers, pursuing the utility of certain ideas, objects, institutions, and the natural world itself through the natural and social sciences, were fond of words like "useful" and "improvement."

As Trevor-Roper suggests, the figure of Francis Bacon (1561–1626) looms large in these developments. The English lawyer and philoso-pher, who held high office under King James I, was enormously influ-ential in the development of modern Western intellectual life. He argued that the primary purpose of thinking was the acquisition of knowledge for the improvement of man's well-being. In his *Advance-ment of Learning* (1605), Bacon even described his central motivation for writing as "a desire of improving."[18]

Some subtle shifts are at work here. We have observed that clas-sical and medieval scholars were not uninterested in transforming the world. But their pursuit of knowledge served the higher purpose of promoting human excellence in the sense of virtuous and holy lives. With Bacon, the emphasis gravitated toward knowing how things work in order to better humanity's condition in the here and now. The concern was thus with usefulness.

Bacon happily affirmed that the contemplation of truth is more "exalted" than utility, but his famous statement that "knowledge and human power are synonymous" reveals his preference for knowledge that can be put to work.[19] Hence, he maintained, the "real and legitimate goal of the sciences is the endowment of human life with new inventions and riches."[20]

Bacon also fueled the development of the scientific method with his seminal book *Novum Organum Scientiarum* (*The New Instrument of Science*, 1620), in which he urged those investigating the natural world not to trust their senses or to begin with self-evident principles. Instead, he pressed his readers to inquire into what was really happening through observation and experiments and then to identify general rules to explain what was occurring.

This is called inductive reasoning. Rather than watching the planets move around the sky and concluding, on the basis of what you see, that they revolve around the earth, you begin with uncertainty. By engaging in many observations of the planets' movements and then conducting experiments, scientists gradually established the falsity of the conviction that the earth was at the universe's center.

It's important to note that this method of inquiry did not suddenly emerge in the sixteenth century. Aristotle had been among the first to hold that truths about the natural world could be discerned through observation and induction. Medieval churchmen like Albertus Magnus also contributed to and encouraged the use of scientific experimentation. Bacon's innovation was the elevation of the scientific method's importance and his argument for using the acquired knowledge to extend man's dominance not only over the natural world but over *himself*. Man must regain, Bacon wrote, his "rights over nature" as we "use all our efforts to make the course of art outstrip nature." [21] "Nature" here means not only the natural world but *human* nature as well.

In his unfinished, posthumously-published novel *New Atlantis* (1627), Bacon is more explicit about this agenda. He envisages a kingdom in which the natural sciences are the primary font of knowledge. At the heart of this new world is a scholarly institution called "Solomon's House"—the implication being that it is the house of wisdom—where men pursue "the knowledge of causes, and secret motions of things" to enlarge "the bounds of human empire, to the effecting of all things possible." [22]

At Solomon's House "new artificial metals" are devised, animals are dissected for the purpose of understanding human anatomy, and men pursue "diverse mechanical arts" and develop sophisticated instruments of war, such as submarines. [23] Here scientists wielding almost divine powers pursue the "curing of some diseases," the "prolongation of life," and even the "restoring of man's body from arefaction"—reversing the aging process—with results described as "miraculous."

All these activities foreshadow the modern university and its emphasis on the natural and applied sciences. But religion isn't absent from the *New Atlantis*. Solomon's House is dedicated to "the study of the works and creatures of God," and Bacon mentions Jews four times, Christians five times, Christ eight times, God nineteen times, and the church once. Yet theology and philosophy are conspicuously absent.

Distinctions—not a divorce

Bacon's *New Atlantis* reflects a religious-like trust in the empirical sciences' power to remake the world. Faith in God is supplanted by *faith* in scientific reason, *faith* in the progress made possible by science, and *faith* that such progress will always improve humanity's well-being.

Bacon himself was no skeptic. His essay "Of Atheism" begins, "I had rather believe all the fables in the [Golden] Legend and the Alcoran [the Koran] than that this universal frame is without a mind." He adds, "It is true, that a little philosophy inclineth man's mind to atheism; but depth in philosophy bringeth men's minds about to religion." [24]

Bacon's *Novum Organum* insisted that what he called men's rights over nature were "assigned to them by the gift of God." These powers, he further explained, must "be governed by right reason and true religion." [25] Scientific experiments and the use of scientific knowledge are subject to the ethical demands of natural law ("right reason") and faith ("true religion"). We should thus pause before proclaiming that there was a radical rupture between the worlds of faith and reason in the thought of a man often portrayed as the father of the scientific method.

Nonetheless, something *had* changed. Perhaps the difference is best explained by the Jesuit historian of philosophy Frederick Copleston. A thirteenth-century theologian like Bonaventure, who embraced the natural sciences as one dimension of knowledge, explored the material world as "a shadow or remote revelation of its divine origin." Bacon's post-medieval scientific outlook did not deny the natural world's divine origins, but it was not primarily concerned with exploring those origins and their implications for the present state of affairs. The chief interest, according to Copleston, was understanding "efficient causality, revealed in mathematically-determinable motion." [26] There is thus a more vivid distinction between, say, physics and metaphysics. Post-Baconian scientists concerned themselves very much with the first, and less and less with the second. It wasn't that physicists were suddenly expected to think like functional atheists. It was more a matter of an increasing specialization in the investigation of different aspects of reality.

Again, these distinctions were not utterly foreign to the medieval world. In the thirteenth century, Aquinas had affirmed that philosophy was a separate realm of inquiry from theology because their presuppositions and starting points are different.[27] There is no denying, however, that the divisions became sharper. In the late seventeenth and the eighteenth century, *very* distinct branches of science started to emerge. What had once been grouped together under "natural philosophy" was gradually separated into highly specialized disciplines such as biology and zoology. Works such as the first modern chemistry textbook, Antoine Lavoisier's *Elementary Treatise on Chemistry* (1789), represented a systematization of knowledge of a particular field.

It is not an exaggeration, therefore, to say that a new canon of inquiry developed during this period, bolstered by the emergence of academies of science across the West, usually outside the church-dominated universities. The Royal Society of London for Improving Natural Knowledge, founded in 1660, became the model for these academies, which provided forums for ideas on a given topic to be discussed dispassionately by specialists and, as time went on, separately from philosophical and theological considerations.

The improvements achieved through these specialized disciplines included the steam engine, pioneered by the English inventor Thomas Newcomen and enhanced by the Scottish engineer James Watt. There was no more powerful symbol of man's growing ability to conquer nature than the hot-air balloon developed by the brothers Joseph-Michel and Jacques-Étienne Montgolfier. Even gravity, it seemed, was no longer a restriction.

The science of man

It wasn't long before people began to take Bacon's hint that they should start viewing themselves as objects to be improved by science. They looked to the new science not only to combat the diseases that had hitherto killed most people by the age of thirty but also to improve human societies more broadly.

One of the most prominent figures of the Scottish Enlightenment, David Hume, expressed this aspiration in his *Treatise on Human Nature* (1738–1740), which was subtitled *An Attempt to Introduce the Experimental Method of Reasoning into Moral Subjects*. Just as there were natural harmonies in the physical world to be discovered through the natural sciences, there were similar harmonies in human society, he believed, which man could discover through the social sciences, such as political economy.

In this confident and optimistic atmosphere, Hume's friend and colleague Adam Smith undertook a substantial rethinking of politics and economics. Smith's most famous book, *An Inquiry into the Nature and Causes of the Wealth of Nations* (1776), was based on almost two decades of study of societal conditions, exploration of historical sources, reflections on human nature based on external observation of men's habits, and the development of hypotheses concerning the underlying causes of men's choices and actions.

Of equal importance was Smith's choice not to pursue his inquiry into the sustained creation of wealth in a study of morality, as Aristotle might have done. Smith treated his topic as a stand-alone subject, thus establishing economics as an independent discipline.

In pursuing a better understanding of economic life, Smith was interested in more than the material improvements that greater wealth might bring. He was concerned with the development of civilization itself. His research was part of the broader project of promoting what he called "natural liberty." Much of the *Wealth of Nations* is a powerful critique of the dominant economic arrangements of his day, which he called the "mercantile system." Mercantilist policies included protection against imports, the subsidizing of domestic industries, state-granted monopolies, constraints on the migration of labor, and occasionally the outlawing of the transfer of new technologies that might produce competition.[28]

Smith's conclusion was that mercantilism was deeply inefficient. Wealth was primarily the result, he demonstrated, of the development and extension of the division of labor within and between nations. The ensuing specialization encouraged economies of scale and gave people an incentive to find and develop their competitive advantage. The result was enhanced efficiency and economic growth.

Smith also decided, however, that mercantilism was *unjust*, for it was premised, he argued, on collusion between merchants and government officials. Politically connected businesses, for instance, were granted legal monopolies on particular trade routes. In return, they lent support to the government. The losers from these arrangements included merchants without political connections and consumers who had no choice but to pay higher prices for lower-quality goods.[29]

In summary, social scientists like Smith, studying the conditions in which human beings lived, proposed hypotheses about how they might behave in different conditions. But their general objective was to identify paths toward freer and more just societies. So while there was a distinction between the empirical aspect of their work and their moral and political goals, the former was understood as serving the latter. *That* was the point of doing social science.

At war with faith?

What did religious believers throughout the West make of the growth of the natural and social sciences and the resulting proposals for improvement? The usual story is that the new learning occasioned conflict between the realms of reason and religion, the Church considering the discoveries and arguments of the Enlightenment a threat to itself and the Christian faith. The truth, however, is rather different.

Over the past one hundred years, historians have demonstrated that it is incorrect to say that devout Christians were universally opposed to the various Enlightenments. According to Ulrich L. Lehner, "only a small fraction of Enlighteners were anti-religious; the overwhelming majority were interested in finding a balanced relation between reason and faith." [30]

There has also been a growing appreciation of the continuity in the meaning and use of words like "enlighten" and "light" from the pre-Enlightenment West to the Enlightenment. Before the seventeenth century, "enlightened" meant that one's soul was illuminated by God's grace. But "light" also served as a symbol for *truth*, whether in Plato's cave or when Christ proclaimed himself to be "the light of the world." Human reason was seen as a reflection of the light of God in the human mind.

While the empirical and social sciences came to be studied independently of theology, Enlightenment thinkers remained intensely interested in religious questions, and not necessarily from a hostile standpoint. Even those working in a field like geology did not set out with the intention of eliminating God from natural history. Instead, as the Enlightenment historian Caroline Winterer writes, "They searched for the regular natural laws that God had set in motion at the beginning of time." [31] God continued to be understood as working directly in history but also, as Newton suggested, in impersonal secondary ways observable by human beings—much as Paul had explained in his letter to the Romans.

There is no doubt that certain Enlightenment thinkers and lines of thought often encountered hostility from the Catholic Church. Many clergymen and laymen worked to place prominent Enlightenment books on the Index of Forbidden Books—a list of texts deemed dangerous to Christian faith or morals and which believers might not read without permission. Opposition from some Catholics intensified as particular Enlightenment thinkers became more explicitly anti-Christian, seeking to diminish and even destroy the Church itself. But as R. R. Palmer's seminal study of eighteenth-century Catholicism illustrated long ago, other Catholics' attitude toward Enlightenment thinking was one of critical engagement. Plenty of European Catholics combined constructive reflection on Enlightenment ideas with loyalty to Rome and resistance to efforts by enlightened monarchs such as the Habsburg emperor Joseph II to control the Church's internal life.[32]

Eighteenth-century French Jesuits, for instance, did not approve of their government's growing encroachments upon the Church, a trend partly driven by Enlightenment concerns for a more rational, top-down administration of society. Despite these pressures, Palmer observes, "In other respects they were men of their time, men of the world skilled in civilized living, and intellectually the most able in the church."[33] The French Jesuits' monthly periodical, the *Journal de Trévoux*, was famed for its objective critiques of ideas and books, whatever the faith of the authors.

In 1751, the first volume of one of the most influential Enlightenment texts, the *Encyclopédie*, compiled by Denis Diderot and a team of 150 scientists and philosophers, was published. In his review of the book, the editor of *Journal de Trévoux*, Father Guillaume-François Berthier, S.J., made some stylistic and substantive criticisms. He concluded, however, by calling the *Encyclopédie* a noble enterprise. The following year, Berthier penned an article in which he pointed out that the *Encyclopédie* contained "over a hundred articles and parts of articles . . . copied almost word for word, and without acknowledgment from earlier works"—including Jesuit publications.[34]

Alongside this type of scholarly and critical interaction, we can even say that there was a "Catholic Enlightenment," which constructively engaged with, among other things, Newton's physics. The first European university to introduce the formal study of experimental physics into the curriculum was the Benedictine University of Salzburg.[35]

Many "Catholic Enlighteners," as Lehner calls them, supported Enlightenment-inspired political reforms without compromising their religious beliefs. The eighteenth-century Habsburg empress Maria Theresa certainly approached government with a greater eye to questions of usefulness than her predecessors had done. She also listened to specialists who could now back up their advice with empirical studies and even rudimentary statistics. Few Habsburg rulers, however, were more devout than Maria Theresa.[36]

These Catholics embraced Enlightenment arguments for greater liberty, pressing for the toleration of groups whose religious views were not, in their view, a threat to the common welfare. Though such toleration was not, to modern eyes, full religious liberty, it marked a considerable advance in a world in which most people—Protestant, Orthodox, Catholic, and even many Deists—generally viewed failure to embrace a country's dominant religion as something close to treason.

Nor did Catholic Enlighteners reject every Enlightenment criticism of the Church. They urged Church authorities to ensure, for example, that the investigation of alleged miracles was informed by the latest scientific knowledge to rule out natural causes. Nevertheless, they insisted that miracles *could* occur. Responding to Hume's

argument that no testimony could authenticate the claim of a miracle, another French Jesuit, Gabriel Gauchat, pointed out that "without
trust in the testimony of men, all human knowledge would vanish." [37]

Openness to the new learning can be seen in the willingness of
Catholic missionaries and bishops to promote practices such as vac-
cination. Eighteenth-century Jesuits and Franciscans even introduced
the writings of decidedly non-Catholic thinkers like Locke and Benjamin Franklin into Spanish colonial America alongside curricula
stressing the natural sciences.[38] In North America, prominent Catholics such as the Carroll family—religiously devout and well-read in
Enlightenment thought—supported the American Revolution and
the subsequent experiment in republican government.[39]

Christian acceptance of the Enlightenment was common in
much of Protestant Europe as well. Locke, a leading figure in the
early Enlightenment, defended Christianity as a rational faith in
his *Reasonableness of Christianity* (1695). But perhaps the best
example of Protestant engagement was the involvement of Church
of Scotland ministers in the Scottish Enlightenment.

With the end of Scottish political independence in 1707, many
of Scotland's religious, intellectual, and legal elites turned their attention from politics, now concentrated in London, to subjects such as
political economy and moral philosophy.

While some Church of Scotland ministers were wary of these
developments, others embraced them. Described by one historian
as "the Scottish Enlightenment at prayer," [40] the Moderate Party of
the Presbyterian church included such luminaries as Hugh Blair, a
minister and preacher at St. Giles' Church in Edinburgh, professor
of rhetoric and belles-lettres at the University of Edinburgh, and a
founder of the Royal Society of Edinburgh; Adam Ferguson, a military chaplain and professor of natural and later moral philosophy
at Edinburgh; William Robertson, an ordained minister, principal

of the University of Edinburgh, historian, and moderator of the Church of Scotland; and Francis Hutcheson, an ordained minister, holder of the chair of Moral Philosophy at the University of Glasgow, and, significantly, Adam Smith's intellectual mentor.

These figures combined Protestant Christian faith with a deep interest in Enlightenment approaches to subjects ranging from philosophy to history. Some of them were inspired to reform university education in Scotland—changes so successful that one of the Moderate Party's primary critics, John Witherspoon, happily implemented similar reforms as Princeton University's sixth president.

The same men insisted that the best of the new learning was compatible with Christianity. Some even incorporated Enlightenment language into their sermons. Blair, for example, told his congregation that Christianity had been a civilizing force, tending "to improve the social intercourse of men, and to assist them on co-operating for common Good." [41] Robertson preached that Christianity had entered the world with impeccable timing, bringing important checks on state power, taming the pagan world's sexual anarchy, and undermining superstition through its emphasis on reason. [42]

This engagement was not uncritical. One of the most illustrious philosophers of the period, the Presbyterian minister Thomas Reid (1710–1796), was very much a participant in Scottish Enlightenment thought, yet much of his "common sense" philosophy was aimed at refuting the skepticism of his friend David Hume. Orthodox in his Christian faith, Reid believed that "zeal for religion" should not lead to the denigration of reason in an effort to elevate revelation's significance. [43] "Revelation was not intended to supersede, but to aid the use of our natural faculties," he maintained. [44] In his *Lectures on Natural Theology*, he cited the presence in the universe of beings with life, reason, and a will as a proof that the universe's First Cause must also possess those features. [45] Intelligence and design in the Cause, he argued, could be further discerned from the evidence of it in nature. It followed that the natural world was created by an intelligent and active Creator.

We find some receptiveness to Enlightenment ideas among eighteenth-century European Jews as well. Indifference, not to mention resistance, to the study of ancient and Enlightenment philosophy tended to be the norm among rabbis of the period. But as prominent a Jewish mind as Moses Mendelssohn (1729–1786), a subject of Frederick the Great, regarded Enlightenment thought, in the words of Michah Gottlieb, as an opportunity for "putting key elements of Jewish metaphysics," such as God's existence, creation, and the soul's immortality, "on a firm philosophical basis." Mendelssohn even credited Enlightenment thinkers such as Locke and Gottfried Leibniz with helping him overcome religious doubts in his youth. He also regarded Enlightenment emphases on God's goodness as his preeminent attribute as a recovery of "a fundamental insight that biblical and rabbinic Judaism first asserted against paganism." [46] Nevertheless, Mendelssohn could be critical of Enlightenment thinkers. Against Leibniz, for example, he defended the idea that God desires the happiness and perfection of every man.[47]

Mendelssohn was not shy about requesting an enlightened monarch like King Frederick to ameliorate the condition of the Jews, noting the inconsistency of the king's exclusion of the Jews from his efforts to advance full civil equality for his subjects. In his book *Jerusalem* (1783), Mendelssohn argued for full freedom of conscience.[48]

Mendelssohn was not trying to strip Judaism of its religious content—though many of his followers did go down that path. Mendelssohn never played down Judaism's religious uniqueness, and he affirmed the Jews' identity as the Chosen People. Even in conditions of religious tolerance, Mendelssohn believed that Jews should obey Jewish law. Like many of his Protestant and Catholic counterparts,

Mendelssohn sought to engage the new learning without compromising his faith.

Distorted reason

Religion's relation to the various Enlightenments plainly wasn't one of endless conflict. Yet certain post-Enlightenment trends, especially the predominance of the scientific method, did weaken the relation between reason and faith throughout the West. The growth of knowledge through experimentation and the material improvement of life combined with the assumption that inquiry should not start with *a priori* principles led some to wonder if *any* knowledge—knowledge of God, principles of logic, etc.—was written into human nature itself.

Traces of such thought may be found in Locke's *Essay Concerning Human Understanding* (1690). Though he regarded human beings as created by an all-powerful intelligent being, Locke insisted that they are born with no "innate ideas." We discover, Locke maintained, how to live with others through experiences and sensations. He consequently held that the human mind is shaped by sensory experiences and that ideas are formed by reflecting upon these experiences. Locke saw this as a largely involuntary process. People were no more capable of shaping or repudiating these ideas in their minds "than a mirror can *refuse, alter, or obliterate the Images or Ideas*, which, the *Objects set before it, do therein produce*." [49]

Such claims about "how we know what we know" sat uneasily with the Jewish, Platonic, Aristotelian, and Christian view that, for instance, knowledge of the truth about good and evil is part of man's reason. They also implied, *contra* Judaism and Christianity, that free will is a fiction. Unfortunately, this repudiation of innate knowledge was not confined to scholars debating "how we know what we know." It gave rise to two distinct trends aptly described as pathologies of reason.

Prometheus unchained

The first pathology flowed from the conclusion that if all knowledge ultimately resulted from reflection upon sensory experiences, then society could be improved by changing man's environment. Human beings, in other words, could be "remade." This view amounted to a type of Prometheanism, a term that refers to the Greek titan Prometheus, who molded man out of clay. In this world, people can create other humans, almost *ex nihilo*: hence, the subtitle of Mary Shelley's novel of 1818, *Frankenstein: The Modern Prometheus*.

Aristotelian philosophy, Jewish law, Roman legislation, and Christian theology acknowledged that rules and laws have a formative effect on men's behavior, and no one denied that people's choices are influenced by their environment. But it is a different matter to hold, as the French *philosophe* Claude Helvétius did, that "education can do anything" and "it is ... only by good laws that we can form virtuous men." [50] The purpose of law, according to such a view, is not merely to restrain evil and encourage the good but also to refashion human nature.

The implications of this shift are profound. No longer is anything "given" about human nature. It is a blank slate, even plastic. Human beings are their own creation, not creatures with an essential nature that, like God's, does not change.

This conception of man generates questions that demand answers. How does one recreate man? What should he be reshaped into? Who makes that decision and assumes responsibility for the reshaping? A common Enlightenment answer to these questions was that the goal was improvement. But this only led to other questions. What does improvement mean? What is its content?

Some Enlightenment thinkers understood improvement as enhancing the usefulness of men and objects to increase the overall sum of happiness. For them, happiness was the maximization of pleasure and the minimization of pain. Others defined improvement as the growing liberation from constraints, especially those grounded in superstition. Many also conceived of improvement as anything that furthered humanity's conquest of nature—including human nature. For most Enlightenment scholars, progress was some combination of these things. As for *who* should be making decisions about the direction in which to reshape individuals and societies, many Enlightenment minds firmly agreed: it should be people like themselves.

One of the legacies of the Enlightenment, then, is the "intellectual" and an associated "public sphere." By "intellectual" we mean more than scholars, such as medieval theologians reflecting upon God's nature or modern physicists trying to comprehend gravity. The term embraces those who study ideas but who also want to see their ideas *applied* to the social order. The "public sphere" is where information is exchanged and subjected to critique by persons and organizations beyond one's own circle. In the eighteenth century, it grew to include newspapers and journals, exhibits and concerts, academies, museums, salons, debating clubs, coffeehouses, and libraries. And a growing number of participants in these conversations came from the worlds of commerce and finance, ensuring a hearing for middle-class opinions about political topics once the preserve of the clergy, the gentry, and the nobility.

Linked to these changes was the growth of what was called "the republic of letters," informal networks of intellectuals who corresponded with each other outside the setting of universities and across boundaries of caste. A king like Frederick the Great could exchange letters on a basis of intellectual equality with Voltaire, the son of a minor, non-noble treasury official. In many cases, correspondents knew that their letters would be read by more than the immediate recipients. Rising literacy and easier access to printed materials enabled more and more people to participate in these exchanges, even at the margins. To be sure, educated men had corresponded with one another before the Enlightenment. But these exchanges attained maturity throughout the eighteenth century and shaped public opinion and taste to a degree that even absolutist rulers could not ignore.

On one level, these were welcome developments. Criticism is one means of separating truth from falsehood and the basis for new and better ways of organizing human affairs. But not all criticisms are valid, and not all proposals for reform advanced by intellectuals are sound. Nor is every opinion that gains ascendancy in the public sphere necessarily correct.

Many Western intellectuals have argued, for instance, that abolishing private property will result in a more humane society. Yet the evidence of the disorder that follows on the drastic curtailment of private property—from the tragedy of the commons to the destruction of incentives to work—is overwhelming. Certain long-standing institutions *do*, it seems, reflect unchanging truths about human nature.

And what happens, we might ask, when some people oppose such proposals for improvement? In that case, intellectuals have a choice. They can work harder to persuade people, or they can insist—because they know better and because those expressing doubts are apparently impervious to reason—that they should be given, or even seize, the power required to implement the changes.

That includes the power to remove obstacles to the desired improvement, and the obstacles might include human beings with different, even contrary, ideas. From here, it's a short step to concluding that the liberty of such persons needs to be diminished so that society can be molded in ways that some intellectuals believe will produce a new humanity.

The path to tyranny opened by Prometheanism is thus clear.

The specter of scientism

A second pathology characteristic of much post-Enlightenment reasoning is often called "scientism": treating the scientific method as the only way of knowing anything and everything.

Few people would want to do without the material improvements to human life that the natural sciences have achieved. With the scientific method, the Age of Reason bequeathed to us a certain power over nature's brutal whims. One side effect of these triumphs was that some began treating the empirical sciences as the *only* form of true reason and the primary way to discern true knowledge. That may sound odd, but if man has no innate knowledge, such as self-evident moral principles, then the conviction that the primary means of recognizing truth is through the scientific method becomes much more plausible.

Few scholars would confess that they were promoting "scientism." It is often a question of mind-set. Bacon's praise in *New Atlantis* of the natural sciences and his comparative silence about other forms of reasoning have more than a whiff of scientism about them. Closer to our own time, the tremendous technological and industrial progress realized in the nineteenth century through such disciplines as biology, chemistry, engineering, and physics encouraged triumphalist rhetoric about science's potential to eclipse everything, as one can see in Jules

Verne's *Twenty Thousand Leagues under the Sea* (1869) and *From the Earth to the Moon* (1865).

On the everyday level, scientism appears whenever the language of science is invoked as a trump card in debate. When someone responds to an argument with "The science says...", he is often implying that the natural sciences provide the only real standard of objectivity, making the scientist a quasi-religious authority to whom all must defer.

Occasionally, scientists themselves speak in this manner. The physicists Stephen Hawking and Leonard Mlodinow begin their book *The Grand Design* (2010) by stating: "What is the nature of reality? Where did all this come from? Did the universe need a creator?... Traditionally these are questions for philosophy, but philosophy is dead. Philosophy has not kept up with modern developments in science, particularly physics. Scientists have become the bearers of the torch of discovery in our quest for knowledge." [51]

Nowhere do Hawking and Mlodinow specify how and why philosophy has not "kept up" with the natural sciences, but they plainly regard science as the only valid form of objective reasoning. In a chapter revealingly titled "The Theory of Everything," Hawking and Mlodinow argue, "The universe is comprehensible because it is governed by scientific laws; that is to say, its behavior can be modeled." [52] The scientific method, therefore, is the key to the whole truth about the universe—or, in Hawking's and Mlodinow's view, "everything."

Scientism's Achilles' heel is that it is based on what philosophers call a self-refuting premise. The truth of the claim "No claims are true unless they can be proved scientifically" cannot itself be proved scientifically. You need to deploy *other* forms of reasoning to make such arguments. But these are forms of reasoning that scientism considers unreasonable.

Even the decision to embark on the scientific enterprise is underpinned by something preceding the scientific method: the reasonable conviction that there is truth, we can know it, and, above all, that it is good to know the difference between truth and error. We don't, for instance, engage in medical research simply because we want to know why penicillin kills germs. We want to know why penicillin kills germs so that we can protect human life and health. Human life, we reason, is good and worthy of protection from disease.

Notwithstanding these serious flaws with scientism, its acceptance has two effects on a society. First, it is believed that anything that can't be quantified is subjective, relative, arbitrary, a matter of opinion, or a reflection of the emotions. The idea of God, then, is reduced, at best, to knowledge of the mathematical structures that undergird nature. This might point to a hypothesis of the type of First Cause proposed by Deists and some Greek philosophers. Outside this framework, however, God becomes a matter of subjective opinion and pious customs—that is to say, meaningless. There is no room in this outlook for, say, Christ as *Pantokrator*, let alone the *Logos* of Philo, John the Evangelist, and Newton.

The second effect of scientism is that it encourages imperialist tendencies in the natural sciences. Instead of dismissing everything unquantifiable as mere opinion, we seek to bring everything under the scientific method. A prominent example of such thought is the use of evolutionary theory to explain morality. The near-universal prohibition of incest, for instance, is explained as an evolutionary adaptation that prevented inbreeding, enhancing the strength of the human species. That's a descriptive position—that is, an attempt to describe how a moral norm came to be established. But it also assumes—for it makes no effort to prove—that no moral knowledge or moral reasoning is innate to human beings.

But evolutionary morality can also take on a prescriptive character insofar as it defines good and evil in evolutionary terms. "Good" is what strengthens the species. "Bad" is what weakens the species.

This thinking underlay the type of moral arguments made by the eugenics movement in defense of such practices as compulsory sterilization of the disabled. Good was whatever promoted better breeding by the fit and whatever limited reproduction by the genetically less well-endowed.

The point to keep in mind is that evolutionary morality is deeply scientistic. It purports to explain morality *and* settle moral questions on the basis of what some scientists believe has been revealed about the human species' development by particular sciences. In 1975, the biologist E. O. Wilson even suggested that "the time has come for ethics to be removed temporarily from the hands of the philosophers and biologicized." [53]

The problems with such positions are manifold. They affirm, for instance, a type of biological determinism that denies free will, including, presumably, the free choice to propose a scientistic theory of everything, reflect on it, and respond to critiques of the theory. Once again, we enter the realm of self-refuting propositions.

Worse, neither scientism nor the scientific method can provide coherent answers to important non-scientific questions, including those posed by the advances of the sciences. Physics has enabled us to develop nuclear energy. Yet neither physics nor the scientific method can help us decide whether we ought to build nuclear plants, let alone deploy nuclear weapons.

We begin to see, then, how scientism, for all its exaltation of reason, unreasonably depreciates reason's ability to know the truth and its capacity to direct man's decisions to the good and the just. Far from representing reason's victory over superstition, scientism is the amputation of reason. We are left unable to ask what are and are not reasonable uses of the natural sciences. Scientism *forbids* us from using our reason to ponder the philosophical dimensions of these questions. Such questions are not put to the side—they are abolished.

Of course, scientism cannot stop such questions from arising in our minds. If people are told that reason is limited to the natural sciences, only to discover that these sciences can't answer important questions, they tend to go down one of three paths. Some attempt to build new systems of comprehending and shaping the world in a manner they consider scientific, burying themselves even deeper in the bunker of scientism. Others conclude that outside science, everything is relative. This conclusion can lead them to assent to the proposition that the only way to make decisions is by turning to whoever possesses the most power and is willing to use it. A third group finds answers by embracing systems of thought that extol irrationalism and unthinking obedience to commands from on high.

And so we confront the destructive forces that the separation of faith and reason has unleashed.

CHAPTER FOUR

Faiths of Destruction

Man is homo religiosus, *by "nature" religious: as much
as he needs food to eat or air to breathe, he needs a
faith for living.*
—Will Herberg

When historians chronicle the twentieth century, they'll surely draw attention to the prominent role of ideas and intellectuals in many of its catastrophes. That includes thinkers who, although non believers, articulated curiously religious systems of thought to which they expected the fidelity we're more accustomed to see in churches and synagogues.

Henri de Lubac, a Jesuit theologian and a member of the French Resistance, pondered these matters in his book *The Drama of Atheist Humanism* (1944). In many quarters, he stated, hostility to religious faith had come to be seen as the true humanist's position. But de Lubac noticed something else: many secular ideologies retained a distinctly religious character. [1]

The Jewish writer Will Herberg observed something similar. Born in Tsarist Russia to a Jewish family that migrated to America in 1911, Herberg spent his youth on the radical Left. Eventually he abandoned Marxism and became a conservative religious intellectual. Known for being one of the first to insist that Western civilization would die if severed from its Jewish and Christian roots, Herberg also stressed that post-Enlightenment ideologies could not escape the influence of man's intrinsically religious nature. They simply channeled the innate human desire to know the truth about the transcendent into this-worldly faiths.

The drift of many Western thinkers away from organized religion throughout the late eighteenth century accelerated in the nineteenth. Certainly there was a religious revival during the same period in reaction to the French Revolution, exemplified by François-René de Chateaubriand's powerful refutation of Jean-Jacques Rousseau and Voltaire, *The Genius of Christianity* (1802).

For every Chateaubriand, however, there were ten nineteenth-century intellectuals who were hostile to religion. For all their differences, Karl Marx (1818–1883), John Stuart Mill (1806–1873), and Friedrich Nietzsche (1844–1900) had something important in common: many of their ideas amounted to pathologies of religion fed by pathologies of reason.

An Old Testament prophet

A German Jew with rabbinical ancestry, Heinrich Marx was very much a man of the Enlightenment. In 1817, however, he converted to Lutheranism so he could practice law in Prussia, and he eventually had his son Karl baptized at the age of six.

Karl Marx's eventual antipathy toward religion is well known. His writings on this topic were underpinned by the belief, expressed in his doctoral thesis, that "in the country of reason" God's existence ceases.[2] Even to entertain the question of God's existence was, to Marx's mind, unreasonable.

For Marx, men's religious beliefs were determined by prevailing economic conditions. As he bluntly stated in *Das Kapital*, "The religious world is but the reflex of the real world."[3] In *On the Jewish Question*, he asked, "What is the secular basis of Judaism?" His answer: "*Practical* need, self-interest." Probing further, he asked, "What is the worldly religion of the Jew? *Huckstering*. What is his worldly God? *Money*."[4] According to this logic, everyday Jewish life throughout an increasingly capitalist West mirrored the economic order.

Turning to Christianity, Marx argued that it dangled the prospect of a better world in the afterlife before people who might otherwise rise up against their worldly oppressors. It was part of the bourgeoisie's apparatus of control, the opium of the people. The struggle against religion, Marx believed, was essential for liberating people from illusions and meeting their "demand for their real happiness."[5]

There was, however, another side to Marx's understanding of religion. He once wrote that it often expressed "real suffering and a protest against real suffering" by the oppressed.[6] Like any European of his time, Marx knew well those scriptural texts in which the prophets denounced oppression of the poor. But Marx's solution remained the same: if you change economic arrangements, religiously inspired protest will disappear.

Marx's insistence that religion was a derivative of material conditions was consistent with his understanding of reason. He regarded the human mind's capacity to know truth as extremely limited. His close collaborator, Friedrich Engels, acknowledged that no one would deny that "twice two makes four, that the three angles of a triangle are equal to two right angles, that Paris is in France, that a man who gets no food dies of hunger, and so forth." [7] But, Engels commented, even in the natural sciences, "As time goes on, final and ultimate truths become remarkably rare in this field." [8] The theories of physicists and biologists, he noted, were always subject to modification and substantive revision.

As for reason's ability to know moral truths, Engels insisted that "it is precisely in this field that final and ultimate truths are most sparsely sown." [9] Moral principles, he asserted, hardly proceeded beyond innocuous generalities and, in any case, were derived "from the practical relations on which [people's] class position is based— from the economic relations in which they carry on production and exchange." [10]

These strict limitations placed by Marx and his collaborators on what reason could know had major implications for Marxist programs for action. The political philosopher Eric Voegelin points out that after Marx decided that questions about man's ultimate origins or the nature of good and evil were futile, he rapidly embraced the Promethean idea of man as his own creator. [11] Marx and Engels spelled this out in a small book called *The Holy Family*: "If man draws all his knowledge, sensations, etc., from the world of the senses and the experience gained in it, the empirical world must be arranged so that in it man experiences and gets used to what is really human, and that he becomes used to himself as man.... If man is shaped by his surroundings, his surroundings must be made human." [12]

Marx was particularly confident that his understanding of society was based on a strictly scientific analysis of history and economics. He even criticized Adam Smith as insufficiently scientific, preferring to "take the sharp edge off a problem" instead of pushing through to reach the conclusions at which Marx arrived in *Das Kapital*. [13]

It's not that Marx thought that human agency played no role. His *Communist Manifesto* underscored the ways in which the bourgeoisie had *acted*: it had "conquered for itself, in the modern representative State, exclusive political sway"; it had played "a most revolutionary part"; and "wherever it has got the upper hand, has put an end to all feudal, patriarchal, idyllic relations." [14] Nevertheless, Marx cautioned that "the modern bourgeoisie is itself the product of a long course of development, of a series of revolutions in the modes of production and of exchange." [15] In the end, economic relations determined people's "consciousness." [16] The scientific conclusion thus remained the same: transforming economic relations would fundamentally alter society and the way people thought about the world.

Marx's followers repeatedly emphasized Marxism's scientific credentials. Socialism was right not because it was just but because it was the most scientifically rational way to organize society and the economy to accelerate Communism's inevitable arrival.

The Marxist theorist and revolutionary Leon Trotsky is often romanticized as a dissenter from Stalin's policies in the 1920s. Trotsky's Marxist orthodoxy, however, manifests itself in his insistence that Communists had to reshape society along more scientific lines. In 1924, he wrote, "Communist life will not be formed blindly . . . but it will be built consciously, it will be tested by thought, it will be directed and corrected." [17] Having extinguished spontaneity, Trotsky explained, "[t]he human species, the sluggish *Homo sapiens*, will once again enter the state of radical reconstruction and will become in its own hands the object of the most complex methods of artificial selection and psychophysical training." [18] It followed that "barbarian routine" would be replaced "by scientific technique, and religion by science." [19]

This highly scientific and Promethean understanding of reason leaves no room for the pursuit of religious questions, let alone assessing a faith's truth-claims. When Lenin began his short book on religion with the words, "Atheism is a natural and inseparable part of Marxism, of the theory and practice of scientific socialism," he was being utterly consistent with Marx's own approach to religion and reason.[20]

Despite God's apparent redundancy in the thought of Marx, Engels, and Lenin, there *was* a type of religious framework at work in the Marxist movements that emerged after the 1850s. Frederick Copleston was more right than he knew when he wrote that one reason Communism did not disappear as most other nineteenth-century philosophies had done was that it had the characteristics of "a faith."[21]

Marx himself comes across as something of an Old Testament prophet, bursting onto history's stage possessed by a grand vision of history and outrage against injustice to tell us what must be done as a matter of right action—*orthopraxis*. Figures like Engels and Lenin enjoy a similar oracular status in Marxist circles.

Like Christianity, Marxism provided a linear account of the goal of history: the New Jerusalem of Communism. This is a heaven on *earth*, but still a *heaven*—the final stage of history in which all contradictions will be resolved and society will be freed from all blemishes.

Marxism thus had a redemptive side, which arose from its confidence that, through science, Marx and others had revealed what drives history and identified how to arrive at history's final phase through a scientific practice of politics. Marxism consequently placed salvation within man's grasp instead of presenting heaven as lying beyond death's frontier.

Marxism also presents a secularized conception of the Christian theological virtue of hope. For Christians, hope is the firm confidence that Christ's promises are true. In this context, hope is not a feeling; it is a virtue that must be practiced and that sustains believers in times of distress, especially when facing persecution and death. Marxism took this notion of hope and focused it on the attainment of an earthly paradise. It became the basis on which many committed Communists subordinated their entire lives to the party and rationalized the imprisonment and killing of millions.

Like Judaism and Christianity, Marxism has its own canon of sacred books—the works of Marx, Engels, and Lenin, among others—which its adherents study as Jews and Christians study the scriptures. Marxists join a church-like organization—the Party—with its own faithful (party members), clerical hierarchy (the Central Committee, the Politburo, the general secretary), theologians (Marxist theoreticians), saints (Che Guevara or Lenin, whose embalmed body is venerated in a shrine), and doctrines from which party members may not stray without compromising their orthodoxy.

Trotsky starkly insisted on this last point in his address to the Thirteenth Congress of the Russian Communist Party in 1924. "None of us," he proclaimed, "desires or is able to dispute the will of the Party. Clearly, the Party is always right.... We can only be right with and by the Party, for history has provided no other way of being in the right." [22]

The more you look, the more obvious are Marxism's parallels with Christianity. Equally evident is that Marxism's arrogation of religious authority was premised upon its radical limitation of reason to the scientific. In Marxist theory and practice, Prometheanism and scientism abound.

A religion of humanity

That Marxists destroyed human life and property on a previously unimaginable scale is indisputable. It was also predictable. For philosophical materialists, words like "dignity" and "rights" are empty constructs, while human beings are simply "material" through which history works. Like any other material object, they can be destroyed

if doing so hastens Communism's arrival. This was the ultimate jus-
tification for the death of millions under Communist regimes. Writing in 1849, Marx stated unambiguously, "When our turn comes, we
shall not make excuses for the terror." [23]

You don't find this type of language in modern liberalism, a
second pathology of reason and faith that emerged in nineteenth-
century Western thought. One of modern liberalism's foundational
thinkers, John Stuart Mill, is usually considered a champion of reason, freedom, religious tolerance, and responsibility for those in
need. There is, however, another view of Mill. As the Cambridge
historian Maurice Cowling recognized in *Mill and Liberalism* (1963),
there was in his liberalism "more than a touch of something resembling moral totalitarianism." [24]

Like Marx's father, Mill's father changed his religion. James Mill
(1773–1836) was a minister of the Church of Scotland before moving to England, where he devoted himself to the study of history and
economics and grew close to the father of utilitarian philosophy,
Jeremy Bentham. Along the way, James Mill abandoned his Christian faith.

In his autobiography, John Stuart Mill observes that he himself "was brought up from the first without any religious belief,
in the ordinary acceptation of the term." [25] But though he was
most likely an agnostic, he retained the religious instinct. Cowling even asserts that Mill's liberalism amounted to nothing less
than an alternative faith, one determined to secure the eventual
submission of nonbelievers.

The phrase "religion of humanity" was first used by the nineteenth-century French philosopher Auguste Comte, who proposed it
as an alternative to supernatural religion. It came with its own priest-
hood, temples, catechism, sacraments, liturgy, and prayers—even its
own Trinity: Humanity, the Earth, and Destiny. It even inspired the

motto on the flag of Brazil, *Ordem e Progresso* ("Order and Progress"), taken from Comte's aspiration, "Love as a principle and order as the basis; progress as the goal."

While Mill's writings are full of references to Comte, Mill did not openly embrace Comte's secular humanist religion. At one point, he even described it as "the completest system of spiritual and temporal despotism which ever yet emanated from a human brain, unless possibly that of Ignatius Loyola." [26] The reference to the founder of the Jesuits hints at Mill's view of traditional Christianity. Careful study of his writings, however, indicates that his liberalism was itself an evangelistic religious enterprise with pretenses to universalism. In his posthumously published essay "The Utility of Religion," Mill even insisted that the "religion of humanity" is "a better religion than any of those which are ordinarily called by that title." [27] Mill did not hide his desire to induce people to abandon the religious myths that science had disproved and to convert to his own enlightened creed.

Though Mill extolled Christ as a great man, he dismissed Christianity as mediocre. "Its ideal," he wrote, "is negative rather than positive; passive rather than active; Innocence rather than Nobleness; Abstinence from Evil rather than energetic Pursuit of Good." Christian ethics was underpinned by "the hope of heaven and the fear of hell," giving "human morality an essentially selfish character, by disconnecting each man's feelings of duty from the interests of his fellow creatures." [28] Christianity's call to a good life was, he thought, no more than urging men to avoid damnation.

Mill was convinced that "a large proportion of the strongest and most cultivated minds" no longer believed the claims of Christianity, adding that "the tendency to disbelieve them appears to grow with the growth of scientific knowledge and critical discrimination." [29] The insinuation was that only the less intelligent and unenlightened would cling to an obsolescent belief system.

Once people had been rescued from their delusions, Mill wanted them to put their faith in achieving the greatest happiness for the greatest number. This is where his father's friend Jeremy Bentham most influenced Mill's thought. Bentham's radicalness lay in his conviction that everything—customs, institutions, laws—should be assessed on a scientific basis, by which he meant objective tests of their utility, understood as the maximizing of pleasure and the minimizing of pain.[30] Bentham even produced a "hedonic calculus" (notice the mathematical language) to help people compute whether their choice contributed to the "sum total" of pleasure. The purpose was to quantify human moral choices. "Disutility" was wrong not because it damaged people but because it was unscientific.

Mill was not blind to the shortfalls of this approach. He recognized the difficulty of trying to calculate how a given choice might contribute to overall pleasure. In *Utilitarianism* (1861), he tried devising an ethics to help societies promote overall happiness by following rules based on a pleasure-pain calculus.

Like others before and since, Mill struggled to overcome the basic error of utilitarianism, namely, trying to measure something as immeasurable as happiness. Mill himself recognized that happiness goes beyond usefulness. He described man as "capable of pursuing spiritual perfection as an end; of desiring for its own sake, the conformity of his own character to his standard of excellence, without hope of good or fear of evil from other source than his own inward consciousness."[31]

If this sounds vague, that's because it is. Plainly Mill wanted to improve human nature. He referred to "the permanent interests of man as a progressive being," but he never explained what those permanent interests might be. Nor did he explain how to integrate them into men as "progressive beings," let alone define what it meant to be a progressive being. But this vagueness did not thwart Mill from stressing the importance of reshaping human beings. Speaking of the working classes in his *Principles of Political Economy*, he argued, "The prospect of the future depends on the degree in which they can be made rational beings." [32] This could be read as a reference to education. But the word "made" suggests that, for all his talk of liberty, Mill wanted to *remake* people, whether they liked it or not, into something different.

Who did Mill consider primarily responsible for remaking man? According to Cowling, the answer lies in understanding Mill's liberalism as a religion. Many religions formally commission classes of people to maintain, explain, and advance the faith: rabbis, ministers, etc. Mill's liberalism, Cowling held, was such a faith. It required and justified what Cowling called a "clerisy"—liberal-minded intellectuals like Mill himself who had dispensed with Christianity and viewed the world through the lens of the sciences. Whether in universities, newspapers, or other culture-shaping institutions, the common mission of the members of this group was to provide "a systematic indoctrination with a view of freeing men from the habitual arbitrariness which prevents them seeing their social duties for what they are." [33] The clerisy were evangelists.

There is considerable support in Mill's writings for Cowling's thesis. Mill unquestionably accorded pride of place to the natural sciences. In his inaugural address as Lord Rector of Scotland's University of Saint Andrews, he portrayed mathematics as exemplifying the search for truth through reason. "[T]there is no intellectual discipline more important than that which the experimental sciences afford," he said.[34] He praised Francis Bacon for establishing inductive reasoning as the primary form of intellectual inquiry.[35]

After paying tribute to the natural sciences, Mill stressed the importance of psychology, languages, economics, and law. Eventually, he got around to stating that liberal education involves exposure to "the principle systems of moral philosophy" such as Aristotelianism, Judaism, and Christianity. The tone was that of one who regards such things as interesting but *passé* and most likely untrue.

But Mill then strongly hinted at what he really thought was the goal of a liberal education. Educators, he said, should not "take a side, and fight stoutly for someone against the rest" in the realm of moral theory, adding immediately, however, that they should "direct [students] towards the establishment and preservation of the rules of conduct most advantageous to mankind." [36] "Rules of conduct," "most advantageous"—that amounts to quiet advocacy for Mill's own version of utilitarianism.

Mill more directly expressed his desire to marginalize Judaism, Christianity, and much Greek philosophy in an essay written in 1836 titled "Civilization." The purpose, at least in part, of civilization was to make men "happier, nobler, and wiser." More significant, however, was "improvement" in the sense of cultivating those things that distinguish civilized nations from "savages." [37] One obstacle to such improvement, he believed, was the pursuit of religious truth by universities like Oxford and Cambridge. Reforming such institutions would require "putting an end to sectarian teaching altogether. The principle itself of dogmatic religion, dogmatic morality, dogmatic philosophy, is what requires to be rooted out; not any particular manifestation of that principle." [38]

The notion that people might have good *reasons* to believe that a religion's revealed truths (dogmas) might be true or that religious institutions like Oxford and Cambridge had a responsibility to explain their religious beliefs to their students was plainly foreign to Mill. Nor did he seem conscious that his own insistence that such things have *no* place in *any* institution of learning sounds itself rather dogmatic.

During his lifetime, Mill was aware that Christianity continued to exert a tremendous influence on the populations of the West. He consequently advocated indirect approaches for minimizing and then reducing its sway. His proposed methods had little to do with scholarly inquiry.

Mill's disparaging asides about Jesuits would have resonated with Protestant Christians and even some Catholics in nineteenth-century Britain. But they also helped acclimatize people to an unfolding assault on orthodox religion. Another of Mill's stratagems was to extoll as the "noblest minds" those who promoted utility and progress. The insinuation was that anyone questioning Mill's vision did so for base reasons or simply wasn't so bright.

In such matters, Mill urged his followers to be attuned to context. In a letter to Comte he advised, "The time has not yet come when we in England shall be able to direct open attacks on theology, including Christian theology, without compromising our cause." [39] But "indirectly," Mill wrote in another letter to Comte, "one may strike any blow one wishes at religious beliefs." That, he said, was how you avoided alienating "the young [...] who would eventually become accustomed to [Mill's and Comte's ideas], including the antireligious ones." [40] All through his correspondence with Comte, Mill counsels a lack of candor, advice that sits awkwardly with the open and fearless quest for truth Mill advocated elsewhere. It betrays a willingness to dissemble that matches that of his fictional Jesuit: one who simulates esteem for others' beliefs in order to erode and eventually destroy those convictions.

The beast awakened

Mill insisted that he "would be the last person to deny" Christianity's contributions to freedom's growth in Europe. Nevertheless, he contended that these contributions were "incomplete and one-sided." Without other ideas "not sanctioned" by Christianity, "human affairs would have been in a worse condition than they are now." [41] There is little doubt that Mill thought that these ideas—by which he appears to mean post-Enlightenment ideas—would supersede revealed religion and induce everyone to embrace something like his religion of humanity: an improved faith for a better, remade, more useful, happier people. That assurance reflected Mill's conviction, shared with Marx, that scientific reason enables man to understand society and reorder it along more rational lines.

It never seems to have occurred to Mill or to Marx that, in his own time, some might come to see *reason itself* as obstructing humanity's self-creation. This is precisely what we find in our third nineteenth-century case of religion and reason going badly wrong: the German philosopher Friedrich Nietzsche.

The son of a Lutheran pastor, Nietzsche was intensely religious as a boy, often remarking that he had the blood of theologians in his veins. Nietzsche even studied theology at the University of Bonn with the intention of following in his father's path. Sometime in the mid-1860s, however, he abandoned Christianity and belief in God. But while he may have coined the phrase "God is dead," the question of religion remained omnipresent throughout his writings.

With good reason, many regard Nietzsche as a chaotic thinker. Many of his books consist entirely of aphorisms. Others view him as an originator of ideas—such as the *Übermensch* (Superman), who rises out of the masses to personify new values—that inspired fascism and Nazism in the twentieth century. These criticisms are true enough. But Nietzsche was intellectually honest insofar as he pursued the full implications of rejecting God.

Atheism was hardly novel in nineteenth-century Europe. But whereas most philosophers who rejected revealed religion believed that reason alone could support their moral system, Nietzsche maintained that when the Christian God had disappeared, anything "built upon this faith," *including* confidence in reason and "the whole of our European morality," would "collapse."[42] He held that if the West rejected Christianity, it would be fundamentally changed, for it would necessarily dispense with the idea of truth and the scientific enterprise in particular. As he wrote in *The Gay Science*, "You will have gathered what I am getting at, namely, that it is still a *metaphysical faith* upon which our faith in science rests—that even we knowers of today, we godless anti-metaphysicians, still take our fire, too, from the flame lit by the thousand-year-old faith, the Christian faith which was also Plato's faith, that God is truth; that truth is divine." [43]

As far as Nietzsche was concerned, aspirations to truth might be useful insofar as people needed to impose order upon what would otherwise be constant flux. That's especially the case, he stated, with regard to language. But Nietzsche thought we should not imagine that language or any description of truth could accurately encapsulate reality.

What's curious about Nietzsche's thoroughgoing skepticism is that he does not appear to have *reasoned* himself into atheism. His rejection of God flowed, as Eric Voegelin illustrated, from his refusal to accept that there was any being, divine or human, greater than himself.[44] No one would call that a reasoned argument. It is a raw assertion of ego and pride. But having dispensed with reason, why should Nietzsche have wanted to think rationally? Why should he have worried about supplanting reason with a sense of his own grandeur? It was logical, then, for Nietzsche to mock those "hard, abstemious, heroic spirits" who rejected God but still sought truth. They were, he said, "far from *free* spirits: *for they* still *believe in the truth!*" [45]

Nietzsche did not view the eclipse of God as a civilizational loss, for he expected the emergence of a higher, nobler, and freer man.

Like Marx and Mill, Nietzsche believed that man had to recreate his own nature, to become the one who realizes that if there is no truth, the only thing left to do is act. "This world," declared Nietzsche, "is the Will to Power—and nothing else!" [46]

Part of that remaking of man involved dispensing with the idea of conscience. Conscience, said Nietzsche, is a "sickness," the result of man's being "forced into an oppressively narrow and regular morality," which is "a place of torture, an uncertain and dangerous wilderness." [47] It can be cured only by acknowledging God's nonexistence and forsaking any idea of truth. In Nietzsche's words, "the value of truth must for once, by way of experiment, be called into question." [48]

The word "experiment" implies the scientific method. Truth is to be refuted by science! But the word "sickness" reveals Nietzsche's conviction that the experience of conscience—and therefore of guilt and responsibility—is a psychological illness. Conscience has nothing to do with truth, reason, or free will. In his backhanded way, Nietzsche recognized that the notion of conscience is rooted in the capacity and will to know truth. Absent truth, conscience can only be considered a burden.

What then was to fill this vacuum? Nietzsche believed that the simultaneous deaths of God and reason opened up a new horizon of choices that were, as the title of another of his books put it, *Beyond Good and Evil* (1886). Those capable of becoming higher beings had to move beyond a "herd morality," embracing values derived not from faith or reason but from a will to power. Nietzsche identified those values in a briskly catechetical format in *The Antichrist* (1895):

> What is good? Everything that heightens the feeling of power in man, the will to power, power itself.
> What is bad? Everything that is born of weakness.

What is happiness? The feeling that power is *growing*, that resistance is overcome.

Not contentedness but more power; not peace but war; not virtue but fitness (Renaissance virtue, *virtù*, virtue that is moraline-free).

The weak and the failures shall perish: first principle of *our* love of man. And they shall even be given every possible assistance.[49]

Nietzsche expresses contempt for the weak while exalting those who seek power. Morality is understood to be the self-created life, free from any constraints of truth. He even offers an example of those who have moved beyond the herd mentality because they accept that we cannot know truth.

From the eleventh to the late thirteenth centuries, a Muslim sect commonly known as the Assassins controlled fortresses across modern-day Iran, Lebanon, and Syria. As the name suggests, the sect's leaders regularly deployed assassination as a weapon against their enemies, usually in public so as to intimidate other potential opponents.[50] Those who gave their lives while performing their mission were guaranteed entry into paradise—the same deal offered to twenty-first-century jihadists. Nietzsche saw the Assassins as "free spirits *par excellence*," deriving their liberty from what he imagined to be their knowledge of the ultimate secret: that "nothing is true, [so] everything is permitted."[51]

Nietzsche was not afraid to apply these convictions to the sciences. If truth is a fiction, and if all "knowledge works as an instrument of power," then the information revealed by the natural sciences must also be derived not from reason but from the will to power.[52] This explains why Nietzsche portrayed the atom as a symbol invented

by physicists to project the power of human beings over natural phenomena. Nietzsche likewise insisted that biological change had to be
understood as an expression of the will to power. All organisms, he
argued, strive to overcome obstacles and fight each other to express
their greater strength.[53] It was on this basis that he attacked Darwin's
theory of evolutionary adaptation. Different species, Nietzsche held,
do not adjust to external circumstances. Instead, the "essential factor"
is "the tremendous power to shape and create forms from within, a
power which *uses* and *exploits* the environment." [54]

There's an obvious flaw to Nietzsche's argument that there is *no*
truth and there is *only* power. And, as we have seen, it is the error
that all forms of skepticism commit. Skepticism assumes there is an
absolute, objectively true standpoint from which we can determine
that every claim to truth is fictional. But the existence of such a standpoint is itself irreconcilable with the human mind's supposed inabil-
ity to know truth.

Nietzsche never showed any interest in answering such criticisms.
He had a standard response to those who think we can reason about
moral questions or who believe that the God proclaimed by Judaism
and Christianity is real and reasonable or who contend that fundamental principles of logic cannot be reduced to the will to power: they
were fools and slaves. Christianity, therefore, was a "slave religion"
that, like Judaism, taught a "slave morality."

These responses demonstrate that, on one level, Nietzsche was
the antithesis of the best aspects of the Enlightenment. He rejected
reason, including scientific reason, as a mere projection of what really
matters—power. On the other hand, Nietzsche was concerned with
casting off the fetters of the past and the chains of dead systems of
thought in the quest for humanity's liberation. In this, he was aligned
with Enlightenment conceptions of freedom: so much so that he
sought to liberate human beings from reason itself.

But in the end, the pastor's son could not escape the religious out-look. For all is not lost in Nietzsche's world. He is *not* a forecaster of despair. For Nietzsche, man is on a voyage, anticipated by prophets like Nietzsche himself, at the end of which lies man's transcendence of his very nature. Nietzsche even posited a savior—the "Superman," though he was not especially clear about what and who this *Übermensch* might be. Tellingly, he did suggest that the Superman would be something like "the Roman Caesar with Christ's soul," or even like a Greek deity who comes down to earth.[55] What's clear is that Nietzsche's Superman is the ultimate goal of the will to power and that he is a fully human, yet godlike, being who will rise up and affirm once and for all not truth, not love, but simply "Life."

The fullness of life awaits us once we conquer our socially con-ditioned inhibitions and embrace, without reservations, the will to power. We should not be surprised to discover that Nietzsche denounced the Christian God as a "declaration of war against life, against nature, against the will to live!"[56] For Nietzsche was pro-posing a new faith: a faith in life, in all its rawness.

Despite Nietzsche's disdain for Christianity, the parallels between the Christian faith and his faith are not hard to recognize. Both see history moving toward a consummation. Nietzsche also speaks of a savior, one foretold by prophets, who comes to life in something like a resurrection. Like the Hebrew and Christian scriptures, Nietzsche's writing oscillates between mystery, poetry, allegory, and catechesis, interspersed with philosophical claims. In his own peculiar way, Nietzsche was just as much a *homo religiosus* as Marx and Mill.

Lessons not learned

It is tempting to say that Nietzsche's ideas came crashing down when the Red Army rolled into Berlin in April 1945 and his most infamous admirer committed suicide in a bunker. Marx's ambitions, many believe, were left in a heap of rubble when the Berlin Wall came down forty-four years later. Likewise, Mill's confidence in an emergent religion of humanity seems tragically naïve given the oceans of blood shed throughout the twentieth century.

But can we really say that the West is now free of Promethean temptations? Has scientism disappeared? Can we say that quasi-religious ideologies no longer haunt the imagination of Western societies?

The answer, I fear, is a resounding no. They may have changed their form, but pathologies of reason and faith have continued their proliferation in the West through the twentieth century until today. Bad ideas have a way of persisting.

CHAPTER FIVE

Authoritarian Relativism, Liberal Religion, and Jihadism

*At the heart of liberty is the right to define one's own con-
cept of existence, of meaning, of the universe, and of the
mystery of human life.*
—*Justice Anthony Kennedy*

It is hard to envisage someone more distant from Nietzsche than a
mild-mannered late-twentieth-century justice of the United States
Supreme Court. But if any remark illustrates how far Nietzschean
ideas had entered mainstream Western thought ninety-two years after
the philosopher's death, it was Justice Anthony Kennedy's infamous
"sweet-mystery-of-life passage" (as Justice Antonin Scalia derisively
labeled it) in his majority opinion in *Planned Parenthood v. Casey*
(1992) reaffirming an expansive right to abortion.[1]

The significance of this passage, however, extends well beyond
the question of abortion, for Kennedy articulated an idea of freedom
that fences off liberty from man's capacity to know truth—truths of
science, truths knowable by reason, and truths revealed by religion.
If he had written that people have the right to seek the truth and act
accordingly (consistent with other people's liberty to do the same and

the needs of public order), his words might have been interpreted as an endorsement of the rights of conscience grounded in humanity's desire to know and live in truth. But the phrase "define one's own concept" and the absence of any reference to truth indicate something different. They make it hard to understand Kennedy as saying anything but the idea that freedom is secure only when a society officially endorses relativism.

People have always disagreed about fundamental questions, ranging from the limits of state coercion to God's existence. Some of the intensity of these disagreements proceeds from people's convictions that their beliefs are closer to the truth than others'. By the end of the twentieth century, however, this commitment to knowing truth—at least beyond the measurable and empirical—was weakening throughout the West as skepticism about moral and religious truths attained an ascendancy in culture, politics, and the law.

How relativism becomes tyrannical

The roots of this thinking can be found in many of the pathologies surveyed in Chapters Three and Four. If, for instance, our ability to reason is reduced to the scientific method alone, then philosophical and theological truth-claims must be merely matters of opinion. And yet the resulting relativism soon becomes not a matter of opinion but enforceable dogma. So how does this happen? Aren't philosophies or religions with strong truth-claims more likely to have an authoritarian streak?

There's no doubt that certain ideologies that claim the fullness of truth have turned authoritarian once their adherents have attained power. More recent examples include the Bolsheviks in Russia, the Nazis in Germany, and Islamic revolutionaries in Iran. But relativism's potential for tyranny becomes clear the moment we assume that *any* philosophical or religious truth-claim is bound to threaten free-dom. Anyone who regards a particular philosophy or religion as true, it is argued, cannot live peacefully with people who hold different views. For if someone believes he knows the truth, then he presum-ably wants everyone else to embrace that truth. He might even be willing to use force to encourage people down that path.

In a homily given the day before he was elected pope in 2005, Cardinal Joseph Ratzinger described this preferential option for phil-osophical and religious relativity as having achieved such dominance that it threatened freedom: "Today, having a clear faith based on the Creed of the Church is often labeled as fundamentalism. Whereas relativism, that is, letting oneself be 'tossed here and there, carried about by every wind of doctrine,' seems the only attitude that can cope with modern times. We are building a dictatorship of relativism that does not recognize anything as definitive and whose ultimate goal consists solely of one's own ego and desires." [2]

In such conditions, tolerance is no longer a matter of establishing the freedom to express one's views and argue about what is true. Instead it becomes a tool for shutting down discussion by insisting that *no one* may claim that his philosophical or theological positions are true. Tolerance becomes a means of banishing the truth as the standard by which all ideas are tested. The coercion at the heart of the dictatorship of relativism follows from the conclusion that we *ought* to marginalize anyone who argues that some ideas are right while others are wrong. Even discussing the rightness or wrongness of people's free choices, then, becomes impermissible. Expressions like "Who am I to judge?" no longer warn us against presuming to judge the state of another person's soul but stigmatize *any* judgment that a certain act might be wrong or imprudent.

The inconsistency at the heart of authoritarian relativism is that, despite its aspiration to neutrality about the truth of philosophical and religious positions, it privileges—legally, politically, and socially—a commitment to relativity about the truth.

One root of this relativism is skepticism about reason's ability to discern any truth other than what is empirically demonstrable. We've seen that this disposition goes back thousands of years. But it was bound to acquire increased potency as unbelief in the *Logos* became prevalent. The Anglican theologian Ian Markham puts this point forcibly: "You cannot assume a rationality and then argue that there is no foundation to that rationality. Either God and rationality go or God and rationality stay. Either Nietzsche or Aquinas, that is our choice."[3]

If we choose Nietzsche, all questions of justice are condensed to who has power and who does not. Public life becomes a competition among individuals to number among those who are (1) powerful enough to get to realize their desires, (2) clever enough to produce rationalizations for their presence among the powerful, and (3) strong enough to trample anyone whose existence or beliefs might limit their ability to do whatever they want. Might makes right.

Whether the reign of the powerful is cleverly disguised or open, its Nietzschean and authoritarian character is evident. And at its root is the relativism that flows from the truncation of reason after the eclipse of *Logos*.

Religions of sentiment

Relativism—the collapse of confidence in reason's ability to arrive at non-empirical truths—has implications for more than politics. It can empty a religion like Christianity of its commitment to rationality. In what is called "liberal religion," God is very distant indeed from the *Logos*.

In previous chapters, we saw how religious believers in the seventeenth and eighteenth centuries grappled with the learning unleashed by the Enlightenment. Many were critical of particular currents of Enlightenment thought. Others saw no essential incompatibility between orthodox faith and the Enlightenment's emphasis on the empirical and social sciences. Some in the West, however, began to rethink their faith and to embrace "liberal religion," a broad term that encompasses everyone from its early nineteenth century progenitor, Friedrich Schleiermacher, to such twentieth-century figures as the Episcopal bishop John Shelby Spong and the Catholic priest Alfred Loisy.

In 1879, the English theologian John Henry Newman addressed "liberalism in religion" in his so-called "Biglietto Speech," given in Rome on the occasion of his being named a cardinal by Pope Leo XIII. His analysis of the subject—the "one great mischief" that he had resisted for fifty years—remains unsurpassed.[4]

The directness of Newman's assault on liberal religion surprised many people. He had been seen as ill at ease with the Catholic Church's direction during the pontificate of Leo's predecessor, Pius IX, and his misgivings about the opportuneness of the definition of papal infallibility by the First Vatican Council (1869–1870) were well known. But those who had followed Newman's thought over the course of his career would have recognized the opposition to liberalism that had been there from the beginning.

In his Biglietto Speech, Newman identified a number of doctrines of liberal religion: (1) "that there is no positive truth in religion," (2) "that one creed is as good as another," (3) that no religion can be recognized as true for "all are matters of opinion," (4) that "revealed religion is not a truth, but a sentiment and a taste; not an objective faith, not miraculous," and (5) that "it is the right of each individual to make it say just what strikes his fancy."[5]

These words demonstrate that Newman saw liberal religion as premised on the same skepticism about reason's ability to know truth that we find in authoritarian relativism. His use of the word "taste" would have been understood as a critical reference to Schleiermacher, who, as noted in Chapter One, used this word to assert religion's essentially subjective character. As Newman saw it, liberal religion was primarily about inward feelings, not truth. Right feelings and experiences were to be preferred to right thought and right actions, any emphasis upon which was consequently dismissed as "legalism" or Pelagianism (the Christian heresy that salvation can be earned through good works).

Relying on Newman's analysis, one can see that liberalism in religion has permeated much of Western Christianity, especially since the 1950s. Entire Protestant and Anglican churches have embraced it, as have many Catholics whose formative experiences were in the 1960s and 1970s and who shared with liberal Protestants a loss of confidence in the realism and rationality of biblical faith.

That loss of confidence owes something to another feature of liberal Christianity of which Newman was deeply conscious: the tendency to regard scripture, the Church, and even Christian faith itself as essentially human constructs. Accompanying this demystification of the faith is a barely disguised insistence that the Church always requires wholesale adaptation to the conventional secular liberal positions at any given moment. The result is chronic doctrinal instability—and thus incoherence—and the degeneration of churches into something barely distinguishable from secular nongovernmental organizations. Such was the situation of many Protestant and Catholic churches through much of the West in the early twenty-first century.

Newman's antipathy to liberal religion, however, also reflected another side of his thought. He regarded certain forms of secular liberalism as alternative religions that embodied fallacies about the nature of reason.

Newman understood the ambiguity of terms like "liberalism." In *Apologia Pro Vita Sua*, Newman's own "history of his religious opinions," he specified that his condemnation of liberalism was not a critique of such prominent French Catholics as Charles de Montalembert and Henri-Dominique Lacordaire, "two men whom I so highly admire."[6] They were believers who embraced the "liberal" label in the context of post-Revolutionary France, a very different political and religious world from the Oxford and England of Newman's time.

We get closer to the "liberalism" of which Newman was so critical in a letter he wrote to his mother in 1829. Here he condemned, among others, the "Utilitarians" and "useful knowledge men," whose ideas were propagated by periodicals like the *Westminster Review*.[7] These beliefs and publications were associated with utilitarian thinkers like Bentham (the founder of the *Westminster Review*) as well as James Mill and John Stuart Mill.

Newman's low view of this form of liberalism is reflected in his portrayal in the Biglietto Speech of the fate of a society as it gradually abandons its Christian character, invariably at the behest of those Newman called "Philosophers and Politicians." He begins by noting their imposition of "a universal and a thoroughly secular education, calculated to bring home to every individual that to be orderly, industrious, and sober, is his personal interest."[8] This is not far from J. S. Mill's view of the role of universities.

These liberals, Newman states, recognize that utility, pragmatism, and self-interest are not enough to hold a society together, so they seek to promote their own faith. Newman describes that faith as an amalgam of "broad fundamental ethical truths, of justice, benevolence, veracity, and the like; proved experience; and those natural laws which exist and act spontaneously in society, and in social matters, whether physical or psychological; for instance, in government, trade, finance, sanitary experiments, and the intercourse of nations." [9] This combination bears more than a passing resemblance to Mill's religion of humanity. But while liberals treat this mixture of particular principles, matter-of-factness, and science like a religion, they simultaneously insist that revealed religion is "a private luxury, which a man may have if he will; but which of course he must pay for, and which he must not obtrude upon others, or indulge in to their annoyance." [10]

It is not that "the precepts of justice, truthfulness, sobriety, self-command, benevolence," etc., are bad in themselves. In fact, Newman adds, "there is much in the liberalistic theory which is good and true." [11] Nor did he hold an "anti-science" view at a time when some Christians worried about how to reconcile the scriptures with the tremendous expansion of knowledge of the natural world. Newman was not, for example, troubled by Darwin's *Origin of Species*. In 1871, he told the biologist and Catholic convert St. George Jackson Mivart that he "must not suppose I have personally any great dislike or dread of [Darwin's] theory." [12] What Newman opposed was treating the natural sciences as the only objective form of knowledge and using the empirical method to answer theological and moral questions that the natural sciences cannot answer. In such cases, Newman wrote in *The Idea of a University*, "they exceed their proper bounds, and intrude where they have no right." [13]

More generally, Newman argued that because ideals like justice and benevolence are so unobjectionable in themselves they become dangerous when liberals include them in the "array of principles" that they use "to *supersede*, to block out, religion." [14] In these circumstances, those who maintain that it is unreasonable to exclude from the public square arguments based on religion or appeals to natural reason are dismissed by liberals like Mill as irrational, intolerant, lacking benevolence, and unscientific—in a word, illiberal.

Mill, I imagine, would be gratified by how many Christians and Jews effectively embraced his religion of humanity throughout the twentieth and early twenty-first centuries. Writing twenty-seven years after the publication of his book *Mill and Liberalism*, Maurice Cowling lamented the extent to which many Christian confessions had collapsed into the religion of humanity and had "become hooked on the politics of the day-before-yesterday." [15] In Cowling's view, their quest for relevance had resulted in irrelevance, save as clerical cheerleaders for whatever happened to be on the agenda of liberal opinion.

But these trends also reflect a crisis in belief among many twentieth-century Christians in the integration of reason and faith, a crisis that paralleled widespread dissent from key Christian dogmas whose coherence depended upon a conception of God as *Logos*. One example concerns the Christian doctrine of Hell, a place of eternal separation from God. Christianity has long taught that Hell is a logical consequence of God's willingness to let men freely choose whether to live in the truth that they can know through reason and faith. In Christian theology, God does not arbitrarily will anyone into Hell, for he loves us and acts rationally. Human beings elect it for themselves by refusing to maintain their friendship with God.

This teaching started to fade in the twentieth century, partly because of biblical scholars who, doubting the veracity of the Gospels, diminished much of the content of these texts to symbols and stories. Hell was subsequently reduced to what the theologian Karl Rahner called "'threat discourse,' and hence not to be read as a preview of something which will exist one day." [16] But if you believe that, John Finnis points out, you view God as a cosmic bluffer—a Divine Being who, like the pagan gods, is deceitful and manipulates people. Such a God cannot be the *Logos* of St. John. [17]

The consequences of the shift away from God as *Logos* are not limited to the Christian church. Because of Christianity's centrality to Western culture, any weakening of its integration of reason and faith and of its view of God as rational is bound to undermine the West's ability to address threats that emanate from other cultures. And one such threat did emerge at the end of the twentieth century—Islamic jihadism—to which neither authoritarian relativism nor liberal religion had any effective response.

Fideism and Islam

Liberal religion is not the only path that Christianity can take once God is stripped of his rationality. Christianity can instead mutate into "fideism," understood as a "belief in the incapacity of the intellect to attain to knowledge of divine matters" and an "excessive emphasis on faith." [18]

In his Regensburg lecture, Benedict XVI noted that Christianity's attachment to reason always ran the risk of reducing Christian faith to metaphysics at the cost of knowing and giving love. One reason many sixteenth-century Protestant Reformers were hostile to figures like Aristotle, he noted, is that they believed the Christian faith had been distorted by an excessive attention to Greek philosophers: "Looking at the tradition of scholastic theology, the Reformers thought they were confronted with a faith system totally conditioned by philosophy, that is to say an articulation of the faith based on an alien system of thought. As a result, faith no longer appeared as a living historical Word but as one element of an overarching philosophical system." [19] This is the background to Martin Luther's complaint in *Against Latomus* (1521), "The sophists have imposed tyranny and bondage upon our freedom to such a point that we must not resist that twice accursed Aristotle, but are compelled to submit. [20]

Protestants were not the only Christians to consider this a problem. Catholic contemporaries of Luther, such as Sir Thomas More and Bishop John Fisher, thought that some scholastic thinkers had reduced the Christian faith to a series of intellectual propositions that neglected scripture and the workings of grace. Such rationalism, they believed, was far removed from the integration of faith and reason achieved in the West by figures like Augustine and Aquinas.[21]

Whenever excessive rationalism appears within their ranks, some Christians are tempted to lurch toward fideism, believing that religious faith is independent of reason, or that faith is necessarily hostile to reason, or that religious precepts require no reasoned explanation for either believers or nonbelievers. The results of such beliefs are a decreasing concern for the reasonableness of faith and a suspicion of philosophy as a corrupting influence. The West's own experience with the problem of fideism makes the failure of many Westerners to see it at work in Islamist jihadism in the twenty-first century all the more astonishing.

It is a mistake to paint with a broad brush when describing an entire religion. Just as there are theological differences between Protestant, Catholic, and Orthodox Christians and between liberal, conservative, and Orthodox Jews, there are substantial theological variations within Sunni Islam and major theological disputes between Sunni and Shiite Muslims. Nor does Islam have an interpretive authority like the magisterium of the Catholic Church or a council of the Orthodox churches that can definitively settle doctrinal arguments. That said, there is much to suggest that Islam, especially Sunni Islam, has long held what is called a highly "voluntarist" view of God. To put it simply, voluntarism accords primacy to the will (*voluntas*) over reason when trying to understand the nature of beings and actions. God's essence, then, is some form of will—a very different view from God as *Logos*.

A thoroughgoing philosophical or theological voluntarist holds, as James Schall, S.J., writes, that "behind all reality is a will that can always be otherwise. It is not bound to any one truth."[22] A voluntarist has no difficulty, then, maintaining that two times two can sometimes equal five. He also holds that God can simply will that what is good today is evil tomorrow and vice versa. This willfulness and its implicit relativism contrast sharply with a conception of God that stresses his rationality and with the idea that both divine and human rationality are bound up with goodness.

Christianity is not a stranger to voluntarist tendencies. The theologian Duns Scotus (1266–1308), for example, believed in natural law and affirmed that God cannot will a contradiction. Wanting to stress God's omnipotence, however, he argued that the will is not always commanded by the intellect and emphasized the divine command as the basis for man's obligation to obey God's law, positions that may reflect a mild voluntarism.[23]

Catholic and Orthodox Christianity, as well as many Protestant confessions, have formally maintained an understanding of God as *Logos*. By contrast, as Robert Reilly underscores in *The Closing of the Muslim Mind*, voluntarism is the dominant position of much if not most of today's Islamic theology.

The ascendancy of voluntarism in the Islamic world, particularly in Sunni Islam, occurred between the ninth and twelfth centuries. The background to this development was the growth of a vast empire characterized by conquest, commerce, and urbanization across the Middle East and North Africa, first under the Umayyad caliphs, who ruled from Damascus from 661 to 750, and then the Abbasid caliphs, who reigned in Baghdad from 751 to 1258. The Abbasids encouraged the translation into Arabic, usually by Arab Christians, of many Greek texts on natural philosophy and the medical and natural sciences, as these were considered useful. In some cases, Greek ideas offered practical solutions to irrigation and engineering problems, while disciplines like logic were deployed in religious disputations with subject populations that had not converted to Islam.[24]

After the fourteenth century, however, there was a remarkable drop-off in the Islamic world's engagement in the sciences. As Hillel Ofek writes, "The civilization that had produced cities, libraries, and observatories and opened itself to the world had now regressed and become closed, resentful, violent, and hostile to discourse and innovation."[25]

There is no single explanation for this change. The Mongol invasion that killed off the Abbasid Empire following Baghdad's destruction in 1258 contributed. The effects of a cultural shock on that level should not be underestimated. Another factor was theological—namely, a longstanding debate between two schools of theology.

The first school was the previously mentioned The Mu'tazilites, who studied Platonic and Aristotelian understandings of reason. The other school, known as the Ash'arites, emerged as a reaction against the The Mu'tazilites' perceived rationalism. The Ash'arites, holding a voluntarist view of Allah, denied any connection between divine or human reason and the Koran and believed that Allah could, if he wished, punish the virtuous and let the wicked enter paradise.[26] For Ash'arites, any science or scholarship that did not promote the religious regulation of everyday life was to be viewed with suspicion.

Gradually, the Ash'arites prevailed over the The Mu'tazilites. As early as 885, the copying of books of philosophy became a crime throughout the Abbasid world. Influential Ash'arite thinkers, such as the Persian-born Sunni scholar Abu Hamid al-Ghazali (1058–1111), the author of *The Incoherence of the Philosophers*, waged a sustained assault on philosophers in general—whether Greek, Christian, or Muslim—and indeed on the entire project of philosophy.[27] Over time, the Ash'arites' voluntarist theology gradually triumphed in Sunni Islam.

The sharp edges of these developments were blunted somewhat by the Maturidiyah school of theology (often called "Maturidism"), which emerged in the tenth century. While opposed to Mu'tazilite rationalism and emphasizing God's omnipotence, Maturidism taught that human beings bear some moral responsibility for their actions.[28]

Nonetheless, the Jewish philosopher Maimonides (1135–1204) was quick to recognize the voluntarist leanings of the Islamic thought he encountered in Spain, Morocco, and Egypt. The Arab Christian monk John of Damascus (c. 675–749), who according to some sources was a civil servant for the Muslim rulers of Syria, observed voluntarist predispositions in Islam at the time of the first Muslim conquests of parts of the Middle East.[29]

Just as Christianity's conception that *Logos* is central to God's nature has powerful implications for that faith's understanding of the nature of reason and its role in human affairs, so too Islamic forms of voluntarism influence Muslim conceptions of reason. Some of this influence has been described in detail by the Jesuit theologian Samir Khalil Samir, one of the most prominent twentieth-century scholars of Islam. In Sunni Islam, Samir stresses, "the argument of authority prevails ('God established this') over that of rationality ('reason allows man to meet knowledge of the moral law')."[30] If God commands x, or if you believe that God commands x, then you must do it—no matter how irrational and immoral x might be. This voluntarist vision of God has also inhibited the development in Islam of a strong tradition of natural law, which offers to all persons, whatever their religious beliefs, reasons that they can accept for acting in certain ways.

Orthodox (small "o") Christianity teaches that all men can know a great deal of truth without the aid of revelation because the light of the *Logos* is reflected in their intellect. Intensely voluntarist positions cannot help but weaken this teaching, for if God is essentially will, the idea of natural law as a reflection of God's rational essence becomes hard to sustain. This is why, Samir states, "it is inconceivable [in Islam] to speak of natural law apart from the religious law (*shariʻa*) given by God to man." He adds, "In the classic Islamic conception revelation comes before reason, prevails upon it, engulfs it." [31]

This is a relationship of strict subordination. The implication is that if God's will conflicts with what reason suggests is right, God's will must prevail—no matter how unreasonable the actions that might follow from this obedience. Such a God is not bound by the qualities inherent in *Logos*. It's easy to see how this type of theology can legitimize the violence of twenty-first-century Islamist terrorism. It also affects the ability of Muslim countries to embrace some central features of Western civilization. A prime case of this is the idea of constitutionalism.

Constitutions are often regarded as the rules, customs, and conventions that determine the powers of political institutions and define a system of government. But constitutions are more than a blueprint for government. Otherwise, it would be possible for a tyrannical regime to comply formally with constitutional law while carrying out fundamentally unjust policies. [32] The Constitution of the United States, for instance, limits the exercise of political authority to promote the ends of *freedom* and *justice*. At the time of its drafting, a major focus was on limiting the powers of individual states. But the Constitution also sought to establish barriers to despotism by dividing power, establishing checks and balances, and specifying protections for particular liberties, especially through the Bill of Rights.

Constitutions do not, however, emerge in a cultural vacuum. One European scholar of Arab philosophy and Islamic theology, Lukas Wick, has argued that constitutional order and the rule of law presuppose a certain view of man, which inevitably reflects the background religious culture. Wick maintains that constitutionalism developed in the West because of Christianity's emphasis upon liberty and natural law.

From the West, constitutionalism spread to other parts of the world—including, as the British-Lebanese historian Albert Hourani emphasizes, many Muslim nations.[33] Wick notes, however, that the adoption of Western-style constitutions in Muslim nations through-out the twentieth century did not prevent major regressions in what little freedom there had previously been in most such countries.

Why has constitutionalism not taken root more firmly in most Muslim countries? Wick seeks to answer this question by taking Islamic theology (of which, he notes, there are many schools and traditions) *seriously*. He does not make the all too common mistake of reading Islam through a Christian or secular lens. He considers, for instance, what theology actually means in Islam and notes that Islam is generally less receptive than Christianity to theological reflection because of its convictions that true knowledge is restricted to revelation and that God's way of being is simply beyond human understanding.

Theology in these expressions of Islam immediately devolves into an emphasis upon action, as expressed in the term *bi-la kayf* ("without how"), and jurisprudence, understood as the immediate application of divine rules to political, social, legal, and economic life. According to Rémi Brague, a leading French historian of philosophy and a spe-cialist in medieval Jewish, Christian, and Muslim thought, this means that "Islam, in contrast [to Christianity], is a religion and a law. Per-haps it is even primarily a law."[34]

Even more consequential is that part of Islamic revelation that runs counter to the Jewish and Christian understanding of what it means for man to be made in God's image. We've seen how the idea of *imago Dei* is crucial for understanding human beings as "co-cre-ators" who share in the light of reason and exercise "sovereignty" in the sense of freedom and free choice. According to Samir, how-ever, the idea that God created man in his image "is absolutely denied by Islam.... In reality the meaning of the adjective 'his' in Islam is 'in the image of man.'" [35] Man is thus considered to be made in man's image.

If that is accurate, then the powers associated with freedom are primarily God's, not man's. One can see, then, why constitutions in Muslim cultures tend to function primarily as power-maps, without also serving, as they are intended to do in the Western tradition, to promote liberty and justice.[36]

To test these conjectures, Wick analyzed reflections on constitutionalism by major Muslim thinkers who had taught in established and recognized Sunni Muslim educational settings. These ranged from outright Islamists to believing Muslims of other persuasions. Wick's aim was to discern whether any of these scholars was friendlier than the others to Western notions of constitutional order. While he found that their overall positions were hardly uniform, Wick concluded that *none* of these thinkers had favorable views of constitutionalism. The difficulty, he says, is that each of them viewed Islamic revelation (which they interpret in various ways) as the *only* source of legitimacy, a view that imposes tremendous inhibitions upon their ability to engage theologically with the Greek, Roman, Jewish, Christian, and Enlightenment thinkers who played indispensable roles in the rise of constitutionalism.[37]

The Iranian Islamic philosopher Abdolkarim Soroush summarizes the problem: "You need some philosophical underpinning, even theological underpinning in order to have a real democratic system. Your God cannot be a despotic God anymore. A despotic God would not be compatible with a democratic rule, with the idea of rights. So you even have to change your idea of God." [38]

Wick does not rule out the eventual development of genuine constitutionalism within Islam, but he does provide a sobering account of the obstacles to be overcome. As Reilly comments, "One might wish this were otherwise, but hope that is not founded upon a grasp of the realities [of Islamic theology and history] will be misplaced." [39]

Wishful thinking

The reluctance of many Westerners to face up to these theological realities is compounded by the restrictions that many Western thinkers have placed on reason. We see this in a widespread predilection among believers and nonbelievers alike to seek materialist explanations for jihadist terrorism—accounts that turn out to be highly questionable, not least because materialism cannot comprehend nonmaterial realities.

After the Islamist terrorist attacks in America in 2001, it was not unusual to hear Western leaders assert that poverty was the primary cause of terrorism. Speaking after Father Jacques Hamel's murder in France by two jihadists in 2016, for example, Pope Francis offered the following response to a question about what concrete measures he would recommend for addressing terrorism: "Terrorism grows when there are no other options, and when the center of the global economy is the god of money and not the person—men and women—this is already the first terrorism! You have cast out the wonder of creation—man and woman—and you have put money in its place." [40] The implication was that economic concerns—the intemperate pursuit of profit, poverty, vast inequalities, unemployment—were driving some Muslims to terrorism.

There is much evidence, however, to suggest that this explanation is simply inaccurate. In a groundbreaking academic study from 2003, Alan B. Krueger and Jitka Maleckova concluded, "Our review of the evidence provides little reason for optimism that a reduction in poverty or an increase in educational attainment would meaningfully reduce international terrorism. Any connection between poverty, education and terrorism is indirect, complicated and probably quite weak." [41]

After examining Hezbollah militants and Palestinian terrorists, among others, Krueger and Maleckova reported, "The available evidence indicates that, compared with the relevant population, members of Hezbollah's militant wing or Palestinian suicide bombers are at least as likely to come from economically advantaged families and have a relatively high level of education as to come from the ranks of the economically disadvantaged and uneducated." [42]

If poverty was the primary reason people became suicide bombers, drove trucks into crowds, slit priests' throats, or axed Jews to death, one would expect recurrent atrocities wherever serious poverty prevailed. But that doesn't happen, suggesting that the economist Robert Barro of Harvard is correct when he asserts, "It is naive to think that increases in income and education will, by themselves, lower international terrorism." [43]

An unwillingness to acknowledge the link between particular Islamic understandings of God and jihadist violence also leads some Christians and Jews to insist that Islam is a "religion of peace." Islam does not in fact mean "peace." Nor does it understand "peace" in the way that Christianity or the West more generally understands this term. As Samir specifies, "In Arabic, *salam* means 'peace,' *salama* means 'health,' and *islam* means 'submission' or 'surrender.'" [44] Peace therefore means a society or a world in which everyone worships Allah, so submission to Allah must be the highest good for all men and women.

On some occasions, Pope Francis acknowledged that elements of Islamic theology lend themselves to legitimations of jihadist violence. "It is true," he stated in an interview in 2016, "that the idea of conquest is inherent in the soul of Islam." [45] Writing in an official capacity, however, Francis maintained in 2013 that "authentic Islam and the proper reading of the Koran are opposed to every form of violence." [46]

Unfortunately, as Samir states, those who assert that Islamist terrorists are acting in a manner contrary to the spirit of Islam "usually know little about Islam." [47] "On the sociohistorical level, from the Qur'an onward," Samir writes, "the ordinary meaning of jihad is unequivocal. [It] indicates the Muslim war in the name of God to defend Islam." [48]

Samir points out one tradition in Islam that accords a limited tolerance to Jews and Christians while dramatically constraining their freedom. This tolerance is not extended to polytheists, pagans, or atheists. There is also, Samir notes, an equally valid tradition in Islam that prefers the verses in the Koran and the sunna (the segment of Muslim law derived from the Prophet Muhammad's statements and recorded actions recognized as binding by Muslims, especially Sunni Muslims) that encourage violence against all non-Muslims. Both traditions, he concludes, are based on legitimate readings of the authoritative Islamic texts. [49]

As for Pope Francis's interpretation of the Koran as opposing all violence in the name of religion, Samir comments: "This phrase is beautiful and expresses a very benevolent attitude on the Pope's part towards Islam. However, in my humble opinion, it expresses more a wish than a reality. The fact that the majority of Muslims are opposed to violence may well be true. But to say that 'the true Islam is against any violence,' does not seem true: there is violence in the Koran." [50]

And to ensure that his readers harbor no illusions, Samir adds: "Those who criticize Islam with regard to the violence are not making an unjust and odious generalization: as evidenced by the present bloody and ongoing issues in the Muslim world. Here in the East we understand very well that Islamist terrorism is religiously motivated, with quotes, prayers and fatwas from imams who encourage violence." [51]

Samir is not alone in making such observations. In an interview in 2016 following a spectacular terrorist attack in Nice that left eighty-six people dead, Rémi Brague maintained that "there is no true dividing line between Islam and Islamism. It is a matter of degree, not of kind." [52] These words—spoken by perhaps the world's foremost authority on comparative classical, Jewish, Christian, and Islamic thought—may be hard for some in the West to hear. That doesn't make them any less perceptive.

Of course, the vast majority of Muslims are *not* terrorists. Like many Christians and Jews, many Muslims are not especially knowledgeable about their faith, and their choices and actions are often at wide variance from Islamic beliefs. Nor are they inclined to act violently against non-Muslims. Millions of Muslims want nothing more than to live in harmony with their non-Muslim neighbors, to whom they wish no harm. Thousands of Muslims have been slaughtered by jihadist terrorists. That said, most of today's terrorists *are* Muslims whose religious convictions *are* a major reason why they torture and murder others, including other Muslims.

We can and should hope that some courageous and believing Muslims will find ways to address these theological problems. [53] But we should not delude ourselves about the scale of these challenges and the sheer difficulty in resolving them. As long as Western religious and political leaders refuse to accept that the dominant Islamic conception of God is presently not one of *Logos* and ignore the voluntarism at the heart of Islamist terrorism, Islamist terrorism will remain unintelligible. [54]

Is the West over?

The predisposition of some Western Christian leaders to favor economic explanations for jihadist terrorism over theological ones reveals how badly the West has lost sight of the importance of getting the relation between reason and faith right. What does this mean for the West's future?

No civilization's survival is guaranteed. Europe is full of archeological reminders of the fallen Roman Empire. There is now much evidence to suggest that the empire, rather than gradually declining as Gibbon supposed, ended relatively quickly in Western Europe.[55] Christianity once dominated the North African coastline, but little more than 250 years after the death of Augustine of Hippo, it was in the hands of Muslim conquerors. Until the 1940s, Central and Eastern Europe was the home of ancient and vibrant Jewish cultures. In just six years, they were wiped out.

If the West's unique integration of reason and faith is a defining characteristic of its civilization, we must conclude that this civilization is seriously imperiled. Ideas that contest and undermine this integration—authoritarian relativism, Prometheanism, Nietzscheanism, scientism, etc.—have permeated every sector of public life. Marxist regimes are fewer in number today, but Marxism's cultural influence persists, especially among intellectuals. So too does Mill's religion of humanity.

Liberal religion may well be dying, to judge from mainstream Protestantism's ongoing collapse, but orthodox versions of Judaism and Christianity struggle to exercise influence upon Western culture. In some cases, they have retreated into self-contained communities or are being encouraged to do so. In the face of Islamist terrorism, many Westerners seem bewildered, averse to accepting the problem's deep theological roots.

Those who care about the truth, however, have no choice. They must combat the pathologies of reason and faith and do so in ways convincing to believers and nonbelievers alike in a post-Enlighten-ment West.

CHAPTER SIX

A Way Back

*Difficulty is a severe instructor, set over us by the supreme
ordinance of a parental guardian and legislator, who
knows us better than we know ourselves, as he loves us
better too. He that wrestles with us strengthens our nerves
and sharpens our skill. Our antagonist is our helper.*
—Edmund Burke

A devout Christian, the eighteenth-century politician and
writer Edmund Burke believed that one reason God permits
evil is to allow good to be realized. Christianity teaches, for
instance, that God allowed Christ's brutal, public, and, by Roman
and Jewish standards, deeply dishonorable death to bring about
humanity's salvation. As Burke watched the French Revolution
unfold, bringing civil upheaval, religious persecution, tyranny, and
military dictatorship in its wake, he surely pondered the import of
that theological point many times.

Yet for all his laments over the Revolution's assault on tradition,
Burke did not think that we could go back in time to rediscover a lost
golden age. Nor was he inclined to regard his Christianity as inevitably

at odds with all the discoveries of Enlightenment minds like that of his friend Adam Smith. Burke was deeply critical of thinkers such as Rousseau, whom he regarded as a father of the chaos unleashed by the Revolution. But not everything about the various Enlightenments, in Burke's view, was antithetical to the civilization that had come before them. A culture can change while maintaining strong continuity with its preexisting philosophical and religious commitments.

Benedict XVI stressed this point in a speech in 2005. Some intellectual currents associated with modernity—most notably a "radical liberalism" and scientism—had long been at odds with Christian faith, he noted. But he also identified two more hopeful developments.

The first was an understanding that the French Revolution's animus against religion need not be the last word on Enlightenment views of faith. Benedict pointed out that the American Revolution and the American Founding offered a different and potentially more constructive alternative.

The second development concerned the natural sciences. Many scientists, the pope suggested, were comprehending the "limitations imposed by their own method, which, despite achieving great things, was nevertheless unable to grasp the global nature of reality."[1] As observed in Chapter One, twentieth-century Nobel physicists understood this problem but were unsure how to address it. At the beginning of the twenty-first century, another Nobel laureate, the economist Vernon L. Smith, proposed a path forward. It was becoming more apparent, he argued, that "what is inescapable is the dependence of science on faith." By "faith," Smith had in mind Paul's definition: the "substance of things hoped for, the evidence of things not seen."[2]

So how might science be dependent upon faith? Smith explains:

> The conceptual and theoretical constructs of science constitute the "substance of things hoped for" and observational

support depends on instruments that record the "evidence of things not seen." As Einstein once said, "It is theory which first determines what can be observed." But I must add, that prior to theory there is what we call "thinking"—a systematic form of consciousness deeply driven by the unconscious that enables understanding and experimental predictions. The parallel is expressed in John (1:1). "In the beginning there was the Word, and the Word was with God, and the Word was God." For humans, all beginnings are in thought or reason.[3]

Just as the natural sciences cannot arise from irrationality, reason cannot arise out of nothingness. We may not yet see it face to face, but in the beginning there must have been the *Logos*. According to Smith, many natural sciences are pointing us in exactly that direction. "[I]n our day," he writes, "the time of the Big Bang, we have come to understand our world, technically, as originating at a massive singularity for which the equations that chart everything from stars and energy to planets have no finite solution."[4] Developments in quantum physics, Smith maintains, have proved "embarrassing" for "classical materialism."[5] The natural sciences, it turns out, now provide us with "indirect evidence of things not seen."[6]

If Smith is right, then scientific knowledge is taking us back in a roundabout way to the *Logos* from which human reason is derived. We can be confident, then, that it is possible for the West to begin reconnecting reason and faith in ways that counteract the pathologies that have been so destructive. This doesn't mean that a quick fix is around the corner. It's not. But surmounting these religious and philosophical pathologies and the West's subsequent crisis of self-belief requires, I suggest, two things. The first is a strong reaffirmation of what I will call the "Central Tradition" of the West and how its critical components fit together. The second is a consideration of what a new encounter between particular threads of Enlightenment thought and the teachings of the Jewish and Christian faiths might look like. One place to begin that discussion is with something that both these religions and the Age of Enlightenment claim to take seriously.

The grandeur of freedom

Enlightenment thinkers were far from uniform. Nor were they shy about criticizing each other. These differences, however, should not distract us from recognizing what they had in common. Alongside the commitment to improvement through reason, Enlightenment thinkers spoke endlessly about freedom: freedom from superstition; freedom from customs and laws that unjustly denied religious, political, and economic liberty for growing numbers of people; and freedom to ask questions that might enhance man's understanding of himself and the world.

Many Enlightenment thinkers attributed the restrictions on freedom to the Church's enormous political influence. For all the anti-Semitism of many *philosophes*, it's easy to see why a Jew living in eighteenth-century Prussia or the Papal States would welcome Enlightenment efforts to reduce the Church's political power, especially the power (exercised through the state) to coerce religious observance. Memories of the religious wars that plagued Europe during the sixteenth and seventeenth centuries also disposed many to favor religious toleration on purely pragmatic grounds. But certain Enlightenment thinkers recognized the evil of compelling people to worship against their conscience and favored religious toleration as a matter of principle.

A case in point was John Locke, who wrote his immensely influential *Letter Concerning Toleration* three years before Britain's Glorious Revolution of 1688, which drove King James II, a Catholic convert, from the throne. Locke's letter was published in 1689, the year Parliament granted a degree of toleration to certain Protestant dissenters from the Church of England—though not to atheists or Catholics.

Locke was not a proponent of religious indifferentism. The word "truth" appears in his letter seventeen times (capitalized eight times), and "true religion" appears five times.[7] But he nevertheless insisted that requiring people to belong to a particular religion was contrary not only to Christ's will but also to what he termed the "genuine Reason of Mankind," which tells us that religious truth that is not embraced freely is not embraced at all.

Locke's opinions about religious toleration, echoed by many Enlightenment figures, would shape America's approach to religious liberty. But arguments against religious persecution did not originate with Locke. Long before the Enlightenment, third- and fourth-century fathers of the Latin Church such as Tertullian and Lactantius had advocated religious toleration.[8]

Many Christians lamented and even opposed the limited openings to religious toleration realized in the eighteenth century. That's partly because the state was widely regarded as having its own responsibilities regarding people's salvation. Others, however, remembered how religious *differences* had turned many Western societies against themselves.

The principle *cuius regio, eius religio* (literally "whose realm, his religion"), established by the Peace of Augsburg in 1555, was an attempt to preempt religious conflicts by proclaiming that the faith of a country and its inhabitants would be the reigning prince's religion.[9] Better to forbid dissent than to allow nations to tear themselves apart in religious disputes. In other instances, Christians noticed that the institution of religious toleration by Enlightenment-influenced monarchs such as Joseph II became an occasion to consolidate the state's power over the Church.

There is little question that the Enlightenment reduced religion's direct involvement in state affairs throughout much of the West, a change that was not without some benefits for believers. For instance, a decline in clerical involvement in secular governance shielded Church officials from the opprobrium following on any government's inevitable failures.

Even more importantly, the Church's gradual loss of political power gave Christians the space to argue that religious and philosophical truth is a better foundation for the Enlightenment value of liberty than notions of "progress" and "usefulness." Few Enlightenment figures would have imagined that one of the twentieth century's most powerful affirmations of religious freedom would emerge from an ecumenical council of the Catholic Church.

In 1965, the Second Vatican Council outlined an argument for religious liberty that was not based on such practical considerations as social harmony and reduced political tensions. Without compromising the Church's claim to teach the fullness of religious truth, the council's Declaration on Religious Freedom, *Dignitatis humanae*, proposed a very different case for religious liberty: "It is in accord with their dignity that all men and women, because they are persons, endowed with reason and free will and therefore bearing personal responsibility, are both impelled by their nature and bound by a moral obligation to seek the truth, especially the truth concerning religion.... They cannot satisfy this obligation in a way that is in keeping with their own nature, however, unless they enjoy psychological freedom as well as immunity from external coercion." [10]

This avowal of religious liberty is based squarely on the proposition that human beings are obliged, because they possess reason and free will, to *seek* the truth about the ultimate significance and causes of the universe and to adhere to their conclusions.

Vatican II's argument for religious liberty achieved three ends. First, it could not be dismissed as special pleading for Catholics. The teaching protected believers and nonbelievers alike. Second, *Dignitatis humanae* dissociated religious liberty from religious relativism by grounding religious freedom in the responsibility to seek and to know religious truth. Third, rooting the right to religious liberty in human reason's orientation to truth placed a stronger limitation on state power than rooting it in feelings, customs, or the preference of the majority would do. For if rights are simply a reflection of emotions, conventions, or the predilections of the majority, then they lack a foundation in reason, and there is no reason in principle for governments to protect them always and everywhere.

A similar logic is at work with regard to a second freedom stressed by some Enlightenment thinkers. In Chapter Three, we saw that a concern for economic liberty pervaded the writings of prominent Enlightenment authors. This commitment helped inspire one of the modern world's first free-trade agreements, the Treaty of Amity and Commerce of 1785 between Prussia and the United States. It was signed on behalf of the United States by three men deeply influenced by the American Enlightenment experience: Benjamin Franklin, John Adams, and Thomas Jefferson. The Enlightenment commitment to religious liberty that all three shared with Prussia's Frederick the Great was reflected in Article 11 of the treaty, which affirmed, "The most perfect freedom of conscience & of worship, is granted to the citizens or subjects of either party, within the jurisdiction of the other." [11]

The importance of economic freedom to America's Revolutionary generation is signified by the attention that George Washington gave to Adam Smith's *Wealth of Nations*, one of the few volumes in his personal library in which he penned a note. Smith himself insisted that mercantilism's restrictions on liberty were unjust, and other Enlightenment writers argued that expanding trade would encourage international peace. But most Enlightenment figures supported economic freedom primarily because market exchanges and robust property rights fostered wealth, promoted efficiency, and reduced poverty.

The problem with this position is that if the primary case for economic freedom was its utility, then it could be sacrificed if an alternative system produced greater material benefits than a market economy. Indeed, many twentieth-century arguments against the free market relied heavily on claims of greater efficiency. In their influential book *The ABC of Communism* (1920), two of the new Soviet regime's leading intellectuals, Nikolai Bukharin and Yevgeni Preobrazhensky, attacked capitalism not so much for its supposed immorality as for its inefficiency. In capitalism, they wrote, "the production and distribution of goods is quite unorganized" and "anarchy of production prevails." [12] Economic freedom, they argued, impedes the "union of production and science," whereby state planners can direct resources to satisfy human needs more efficiently. [13]

As in the case of religious liberty, however, religious believers have produced arguments for a principled right to economic freedom based on what human beings *are* rather than on mere utility. For Jews and Christians, the roots of this position are found in Genesis, where God tells the man to "fill the earth and subdue it" (Genesis 1:28). This call to shape the material world is directly linked to the idea that man bears the image of God (Genesis 1:26). As previously observed, this image is found in man's reason and free will. Nonbelievers can recognize these characteristics as making men "god-like" in the sense of fundamentally different from other animals.

Possessing these unique attributes, only human beings, apart from God, can be creative and thus initiate economic acts. For this reason, Pope John Paul II pointed out that "besides the earth, man's principal resource is *man himself*. His intelligence enables him to discover the earth's productive potential and the many different ways in which human needs can be satisfied." [14] Through the free exercise of their intelligence, human beings not only shape the material world and make it productive but also form themselves in virtues, especially those associated with commercial activity, such as prudent risk-taking and promise-keeping.

Once we recognize that economic freedom is based on certain powers inherent in human beings—powers with a religious explanation but which are also self-evident through the exercise of human reason—we establish an important limit upon state power. Governments now have to produce very good reasons to circumscribe people's exercise of their reason, free choice, and creativity in the economy. Economic freedom is no more absolute than religious freedom. But because it is essential both as a bulwark against despotism and for people to realize their full human potential, the presumption in favor of economic freedom rests on grounds far more compelling than simple efficiency and utility.

Four civilizational theses

The cases for religious and economic freedom exemplify how certain liberties which acquired such momentum in the Enlightenment can be given firmer roots through an encounter with the religious traditions of the West—traditions that have not always been friendly to either religious or economic freedom. To that extent, we can say that the flowering of these two freedoms took place as reason and faith corrected and refined each other.

But the restoration of a healthy integration of faith and reason needs more than this mutual critique and modification. It requires a reestablishment of the very foundations of this integration. This was attempted in the most unexpected of settings—the First Vatican Council—at a time when the forces of religion and the Enlightenment seemed most at loggerheads.

On December 8, 1869, the fiercely anti-modern Pope Pius IX convened six hundred of the world's Catholic bishops in the first ecumenical council since the sixteenth century. The following July, they defined the doctrine of papal infallibility in the dogmatic constitution *Pastor aeternus*. No idea could have been more alien to nineteenth-century liberal opinion, which was increasingly skeptical about religion. The intensity of the debates within and outside the Church about papal infallibility, however, diverted attention from the council's other decree, issued two months earlier, which was, in some respects, far more consequential.

The decree *Dei Filius* forthrightly addressed what it called the widespread denial of man's "rational nature" and affirmed not only that God exists but also that this God can be known *by reason alone*: "God, the source and end of all things, can be known with certainty from the consideration of created things, by the natural power of human reason: ever since the creation of the world, his invisible nature has been clearly perceived in the things that have been made." [15]

Certainly the fullness of knowledge of this same God, the council fathers cautioned, is found only in divine revelation. Faith is above reason. But "there can never be any real disagreement between faith and reason, since it is the same God who reveals the mysteries and infuses faith, and who has endowed the human mind with the light of reason." [16]

Revelation, *Dei Filius* explains, is God's disclosure to men, through acts or propositions, of truths that they could not reach on their own—the Trinitarian nature of God, for example—or that they could comprehend only with difficulty. Once these truths are made known, however, human reason can contemplate them, discerning how they relate to the knowledge that our reason can attain under its own power.

Dei Filius goes on to stress that Christianity supports "the development of human arts and studies," that the Church is "neither ignorant nor contemptuous of the advantages" derived from the natural and social sciences, and that Christians have long recognized that these disciplines must follow their "own proper principles and method."[17] *Dei Filius* thus preempts any accusation that Christianity is hostile to the empirical sciences, non-theological intellectual disciplines, or inductive reasoning.

All the same, Vatican I was making an important point: reason goes beyond the empirical, so much so that it can know the ultimate source of human rationality precisely because reason itself is derived from that same origin. We have already seen that this line of argument is not peculiarly Christian. Moreover, it is an essential part of the Central Tradition—that persistent and particular pattern of human thought and action that has been transmitted across time and has made the West what it is.

In a lecture delivered at the Catholic University of Argentina in 2013, John Finnis identified four of the "superior, sounder theses" that form the core of this tradition.[18] These propositions developed over time and, taken together and never cut off from one another, distinguish the West from other cultures. Though aspects of these theses can be found outside Western societies, it is much harder to find this specific combination of ideas elsewhere. Finnis's four theses are creation, freedom, justice, and faith. They are, he writes, "truths that none of us can afford to take merely for granted."[19] And that is why they require restating.

Creation

In his posthumous autobiography, apparently written between May and August 1876, Charles Darwin cited "the extreme difficulty or rather impossibility of conceiving this immense and vast universe, including man with his capacity for looking far backwards and far into futurity, as the result of blind chance or necessity. When thus reflecting I feel compelled to look to a First Cause having an intelligent mind in some degree analogous to that of man; and I deserve to be called a Theist." [20]

Over time, Darwin tells his readers, his confidence in this thesis of a Creator weakened. "This conclusion," he stated, "has very gradually with many fluctuations become weaker." [21] At some point, Darwin concluded, "The mystery of the beginning of all things is insoluble by us; and I for one must be content to remain an Agnostic." [22]

Darwin was not being entirely candid, however. The research of the theologian and physicist Stanley Jaki shows that Darwin became obsessed with providing a scientific and credible account for the human species' origins that *disposed* of any general or particular act of creation by a divine Creator and replaced it with a purely mechanical and exclusively material description. [23] As Cardinal Christoph Schönborn remarks, "very little doubt remains that with his scientific theory Darwin wanted to help bring about the victory of materialism." [24] To that extent, Darwin was more ideologue than scientist: the ideological objective being to dispense with concepts such as purpose, design, and ends.

Still, for all his anxiousness to propagate a materialist account for his scientific observations, Darwin found it difficult to deny creation: that there is a First Cause Creator and that this Creator is neither an abstract hypothesis nor a being who sets things in motion and then becomes eternally passive. Instead it is, to repeat Darwin's words, "an intelligent mind in some degree analogous to man."

Albert Einstein took a similar position. He did not believe in the God of his ancestors or in Jesus of Nazareth, but he described himself "as a deeply religious man" inasmuch as he was convinced that the laws of nature reveal "an intelligence of such superiority that, compared with it, all the systematic thinking and acting of human beings is an utterly insignificant reflection." [25]

One major implication of the creation thesis is that the natural world is not God, a jumble of competing gods, or endlessly chaotic. A second consequence is that, because human intelligence is "analogous" to that of the Creator, human beings can understand the order that permeates the natural world and shape it. Without this starting point, we are stuck in the dead end of materialism.

By "materialism," I do not mean the hunger to possess and endlessly consume more and more things. Instead I have in mind something we observed when analyzing the underpinnings of Marx's thought—the conviction that everything, including reason, is a product of the material world, that at the root of everything is not a Creator, Intellect, or *Logos* that freely chooses to bring the material world into being and sustain it. There is just material. While there are many philosophical variations of materialism, they all share this foundational claim.

Materialist explanations for reality go back at least as far as Democritus. And their longevity isn't surprising, because the moment you question the creation thesis and start to regard everything as a product of chance, cunning, necessity, adaptation to random circumstances, or some combination of these, the only alternative account of the ultimate foundations of everything is some variant of materialism.

That has serious implications for the West and humanity as a whole. For if human beings have developed by chance—that is, from arbitrary material causes such as atoms randomly smashing against each other—it becomes hard to assert that human life has any meaning or logic beyond our own desires. Nor can we claim that there is any objective standard of good and evil. In the face of an abomination like Auschwitz, a convinced materialist has, strictly speaking, nothing to say beyond observations of a mechanical and empirical nature. When Auschwitz's best-known commandant, Rudolf Höss, described the camp in his memoirs as a remarkable technical accomplishment, he inadvertently underlined this very point.[26]

Nor can consistent materialists hold that there is anything essentially different between a random pile of rocks and the Parthenon in Athens. They have no reason in principle to care about Western civilization—or any civilization. Even reason is reduced to a mere outgrowth of the material.

The more, however, one reflects upon materialism, the greater its implausibility. Materialists cannot deny, for example, that the natural sciences rely heavily on a presumption of order and intelligibility. Every day, scientists seek *explanation*, describe in *words* what they have found, attempt to *demonstrate* how it *relates* to what is already *known*, *reflect* upon and *respond* to *criticism* of the *logic* of the *theoretical* explanations they *give* to their findings, and *search* for—and *find*—directionality in the order of things.

And insofar as materialism involves denial of design, materialists cannot account for the order we *do* find in the universe. Many materialists, for instance, model the human mind on computers. Just as the logic of computers is a product of their material composition and circuitry, so too, they say, is the human mind the product of its biological brain. Yet this analogy ignores the fact that computers do not emerge from nowhere. Information technology has been *designed* by human beings using their reason and freely choosing to do so. A materialist might respond that the human minds that designed and built computers emerged through evolution. But a materialist understanding of evolution cannot account for one of reason's defining features—its *non-material* character. A consistent materialist therefore cannot provide an ultimate account for the *order* we find in information technology.[27]

Materialists often point to the disorder around us—that which *seems* to be purposeless, inefficient, stupid, needlessly complex, and so on—as proof that there is no design and thus no designer. But such arguments assume that because *I* don't understand all or part of what is happening in a given situation, then *everything* must be random and thus proof that there is no design in creation, let alone a designer.

That is a conclusion unsupported by its premise. It is true that not everything is always or immediately comprehensible to the human mind. But something incomprehensible to us *is* intelligible to the mind that is capable of creating the universe out of nothing. Granted, that's not likely to assuage the grief of a parent whose child has inexplicably perished in an earthquake and who is wondering how a good God could allow such a death to happen. Yet it *is* a response that coheres with the logic of the creation thesis and its assertion that there is a rational, intelligent, and omnipotent creator.

Freedom

We have already dealt at length with the second thesis of the West—freedom. The radical freedom of the will, only partially grasped by Greek philosophers and first clearly voiced by the Hebrew prophets, was stressed by Latin and Greek Christians who developed this insight over time with the assistance of Greek and Roman thought.

By "radical freedom of the will," we mean that people really *are* self-directed and self-determining and therefore *responsible* for their free choices. This thesis contrasts with the fatalism of the ancients, with the materialist philosophies of their world and ours, with the soft determinism of Mill (we imagine we are acting freely but we are really not), and with the hard determinism of Marx (our choices are ultimately determined by the dialectics of history).

We all know from experience that some acts are attributable to *nothing else* but our free choice—just as the Creator freely chose to bring creation into being when nothing compelled the Creator to do so. We either choose to follow our reason and do what is good, or we refuse to follow it and do the opposite.

Without this understanding of the *reality* of freedom, there is no accountability for our choices, conscience becomes a fiction that we cannot really explain *as* conscience, and the very idea of freedom for excellence becomes an illusion. Without conscience, personal responsibility, and man's ability to choose between excellence and decadence, Western civilization would come to an end.

Justice

If creation and freedom are understood in the way just described, it becomes impossible to view justice simply as "whatever the law happens to say" at a given time. Nor can justice be seen primarily as a reflection of emotions, guilt, customs, or an anxiousness to appease the economically disadvantaged. Instead justice is the choice of individuals and communities to fulfill their responsibility to give others what is their due: what they are owed as a matter of *reasonableness*.

One source of the Central Tradition's idea of justice is Greek. Plato understood justice as speaking the truth and paying your debts.[28] He also spent time refuting the idea that justice is whatever is to the advantage of the stronger.[29] In other places, Plato presented justice as a master

virtue for individuals and communities, the focus being on the fulfill-
ment of responsibilities.[30]

Aristotle's position was similar. He saw justice as an individual
virtue and also as a virtue that should shape political arrangements.
In the latter case, justice becomes a general moral principle that
underpins the workings of the polis.[31] Many of these Platonic and
Aristotelian ideas were further developed in Roman law.[32]

Plato's and Aristotle's conceptions of justice were challenged by
the philosophers' great rivals, Epicurus and his followers. The premise of justice from an Epicurean standpoint was that happiness is
found in the pursuit of pleasure. Justice was understood as the disposition to leave people undisturbed as far as possible so that everyone
can freely pursue his desires, which meant keeping one's agreements
and not violating the prevailing social norms.[33]

Epicurean and similar conceptions of justice clashed not only
with Aristotle but also with the second major source of the Central
Tradition's idea of justice: the revelation to the Jewish people that
there is one transcendent, intelligent, and intelligible God to whom
all are ultimately accountable for their free choices.[34]

The Decalogue, for example, enumerates *obligations* to act in ways
that promote certain goods (e.g., worship of the true Creator, honor-
ing one's parents) and never directly to choose to damage other goods
(e.g., human life, property). The power of this conception of justice is
that while the Hebrew scriptures stress that these commands come
from God, they are also presented as signs of "wisdom," "righteousness," and "understanding" (Deuteronomy 4:1–6) that other nations
will recognize as wise and righteous. In other words, the commandments are universally true and right and thus *knowable* by non-Jews.
It was against this background that Christianity affirmed the Decalogue as always knowable by and binding on those who have never

heard of Yahweh or Jesus of Nazareth because its precepts are ascertainable by natural reason.

These religious contributions to the West's conception of justice were profound. They applied the requirements of justice equally to everyone: Jew and Gentile, man and woman, rich and poor. There were no "super-humans" who received legal privileges or "sub-humans" who were rightly denied justice. It became ever clearer that, despite their natural differences, all men were owed equal treatment by the law and that legal systems had to meet certain standards to be considered just. That is how we arrived at the idea of the rule of law.

Christianity, however, also taught charity, an emphasis that reinforced justice but which also ensured that the West did not forget that justice is not the full solution to every human problem.

The Gospel of Matthew (22:36–40) records Jesus as responding to the question "Teacher, which commandment is the greatest?" with the following words: "He said to him, 'You shall love the Lord, your God, with all your heart, with all your soul, and with all your mind. This is the greatest and the first commandment. The second is like it: You shall love your neighbor as yourself. The whole law and the prophets depend on these two commandments.'"

Jesus first quotes Deuteronomy 6:5 on loving God and then Leviticus 19:18 on loving one's neighbor. When we look at the verse from Leviticus, we notice that it is surrounded by the Decalogue and other moral and legal instructions, ranging from an insistence upon the impartial administration of justice—"You shall not act dishonestly in rendering judgment. Show neither partiality to the weak nor deference to the mighty, but judge your fellow men justly" (19:15)—to prohibitions against fraud, deception, lying under oath, and, revealingly, hating others. Christ's words make it clear that love is not sentimentality. If you love others, you will act justly and therefore reasonably toward others.

But Christ's commandment to love also reminded his listeners that, in many instances, justice is not enough. To be fully human, we need to go beyond, though without ever nullifying, the requirements of justice. For Christians, Christ's death on the cross in atonement for humanity's sins is the model. Justice is served, but God's love for men is why it occurs in this particular way.

In practical terms, the commandment to love others moved Christians to care for others—Christian and non-Christian alike—on an unprecedented scale, in striking contrast to the pagan cultures of Greece and Rome. Pagan temples occasionally provided some medical help,[35] and the Romans established hospitals of sorts, though access was often limited to members of the domestic households of prominent people and, in other cases, to ill and wounded legionaries.[36]

The Christians were driven to surpass these limitations by their religion's emphasis on self-giving love. The building of hospitals to serve the general population was mandated by the Church from the Council of Nicaea (AD 325) onward. They provided medical help on a previously unimaginable scale, especially in the Byzantine Empire,[37] to all comers and with a specific focus on those who received little attention in the pagan world, including the poor, the disabled, women, slaves, and non-citizens.[38]

This was just one way in which Christians responded to forms of human suffering for which justice was not a sufficient response. Expressions of charity supplemented the attention to justice and steadily worked their way into Western culture. It is unlikely that such practices would have emerged from the thought of Aristotle and Plato, and it is clear that they could not have been derived from Epicurus's view of justice.

Faith

This attention to the ways in which the Jewish and Christian faiths shaped and supplemented the idea of justice brings us to the last of the four theses Finnis identifies as part of the Central Tradition.

When people hear the word "faith," they often think of the expression "leap of faith," which suggests that one must jump over a vast chasm separating reason from faith. The expression sometimes implies that faith is beyond or even opposed to reason, that only a blind act of will can bring a person to religious belief.

Orthodox Christianity's conception of religious faith is utterly different. Long before Vatican I, Christians insisted that faith was rational, not least because, as Finnis writes, it "is a matter of believing in the truth of propositions held out to us for a fully reasonable judgment." [39] The free choice to believe in particular propositions—for example, that God is the Creator or that God wills the good of men, who can make free choices—is considered reasonable because those propositions are judged to have been revealed by God himself: first, to chosen individuals (the Hebrew prophets) among a chosen people and, ultimately, in the life and deeds of Jesus of Nazareth.

Faith in this sense is *knowing* the fullness of truth. Some of this information is attainable only through revelation; it cannot be discerned by reason alone. But this kind of knowledge is not inconsistent with rational inquiry into truth.

Those truths of Christianity that are known by faith—the Incarnation, for instance—are not presented or understood as legends. If anything characterizes the prophets of Israel and the authors of the Christian Gospels, it is a thirst to get *beyond* myth and arrive at knowledge of the truth. The scriptures seek to answer Pontius Pilate's question *Quid est veritas*? ("What is truth?") with the full truth about reality.

The same texts strive to provide evidence that we have good reason to believe in the truthfulness and authority of the one who reveals the truth. One such proof is the miracles recorded in the scriptures. The authors of the Gospels repeatedly emphasize that Christ's miracles were *witnessed* by people with no reason to lie, bewilder, or mislead. The same authors intended this information to be transmitted to other persons whose reason enabled them to judge whether the information was credible.

This doesn't mean that faith can be attained only by rational reflection on the claims of the Hebrew and Christian scriptures. Over the centuries, many Jews and Christians have attested that they came to religious faith through an experience they understand as revealing to them the truth of God's existence—and not just any god, but the God of the Bible. But attaining faith through such experiences does not contradict efforts to engage the truths of faith with the insights of reason.

According to the Acts of the Apostles, Paul was transformed from a determined persecutor of the first communities of the followers of Jesus into Christianity's greatest advocate through a powerful experience of the risen Jesus of Nazareth (Acts 9:1–31). That encounter, however, did not inhibit Paul from engaging in philosophical discussions with Greeks and Romans (Acts 17:16–34). Nor did it impede him from arguing that the moral truths stated in the Decalogue were also discernible through reason.

Likewise, the author of the Gospel of John records that the Beloved Disciple had the profound experience of seeing the empty tomb and believing even before the risen Jesus appeared to his disciples (John 20:1–8). Yet the same author did not refrain from using the Hellenic and Hellenized-Jewish concept of *Logos* to convey theological and philosophical insights into God's nature to those who heard or read this Gospel.

So what might this thesis of faith mean for those in the West who are not believing Jews and Christians but who still think Western civilization is a stupendous achievement worth preserving? One answer might go along the following lines.

First, many people of good will in the West are uncertain that the religious claims of Judaism and Christianity are true. Some doubt

God's very existence. Yet neither disposition precludes these same people from recognizing Judaism and Christianity as the most consistent transmitters of the four theses—creation, freedom, justice, and faith—that are at the core of the West's identity. The concession of the Italian philosopher Benedetto Croce (1866–1952) that "it is impossible for us to call ourselves completely non-Christians" expressed one prominent nonbeliever's recognition that the West cannot escape its religious roots.[40]

Second, the same nonbelievers can affirm that these two religious traditions have, in different ways and to varying degrees, taken reason seriously and contributed to the foundations of the natural sciences so prized by the Enlightenment. On this basis, nonbelievers can join those believing Jews and Christians who have not embraced liberal religion in posing serious questions about Western civilization's compatibility with philosophies and faiths that have a low view of reason.

Third, the nonbeliever's religious difficulties and doubts are no obstacle to appreciating the dangers of separating reason from faith and forbidding reason to explore the questions that arise from religious faith. One does not have to believe in God to recognize that putting reason and faith in opposition to each other has encouraged the pathologies identified throughout this book. One need not be a convinced Christian or Jew to understand that pathologies of reason and faith are behind the pseudo-religion of Marxism and the narrowing of reason's horizons to scientism.

A delicate tapestry

The West's integration of creation, freedom, justice, and faith is always fragile, and undermining any one of them undercuts the others. Without creation, the intelligibility of the universe is hard to sustain. Without intelligibility, freedom is only a mirage, justice a sophism, and faith nothing more than emotivism or ideology. If freedom is meaningless, people cannot be held responsible for their actions. Without personal responsibility, there is no true justice. Without justice, the existence of an intelligent Creator to whom all must eventually answer is thrown into doubt.

The same logic, however, works the other way. If we reason and consequently conclude that there is a *Logos*, one who remains involved in his creation, then outlooks such as fideism, liberal religion, scientism, and materialism, as well as the philosophies of Marx, Mill, and Nietzsche, are untenable. We can also argue that there *is* justice, and that it is not simply whatever the influential and powerful want it to be.

Again and again, we see that belief in the *Logos*—or at least an acknowledgment that it is a more plausible position than assertions that all is flux or that everything begins in nothingness—is crucial for preserving the West's civilizational achievements from the rule and consequences of irrationality. Few have explained the need for this type of enlightenment better than someone who experienced the full force of the power of senselessness and all its implications in a land where unreason triumphed beyond anyone's expectations.

CHAPTER SEVEN

On Earth as in Heaven

*The liberal and secularized state lives on premises that it
cannot itself guarantee. On the one hand, it can subsist
only if the freedom it [grants] to its citizens is regulated
from within, inside the moral substance of individuals and
of a homogeneous society. On the other hand, it is not able
to guarantee these forces of inner regulation by itself without renouncing its liberalism.*
—*Ernst-Wolfgang Böckenförde*

Named after its author, a German intellectual and judge who
grew up in Nazi Germany, the "Böckenförde Dilemma"
neatly summarizes the trap in which much of the post-
Enlightenment West finds itself. Having developed and secularized a
range of freedoms that originated in its pre-Enlightenment heritage,
the West has found it difficult to maintain the moral ballast needed
to sustain such liberties.

Even the German philosopher Jürgen Habermas, a self-described
methodological atheist and one of the twentieth century's leading
representatives of Enlightenment thought, acknowledged that the

two religious faiths of the West are among the major sources of such moral capital.[1] But therein lies the dilemma: The moment that secular Western states appeal to these sources, they seemingly violate their commitment to secularity and call into question the sufficiency of post-Enlightenment conceptions of reason. Doubts about that sufficiency are reinforced by the fact that post-Enlightenment societies were among those that succumbed in the twentieth century to movements promoting "the class" or "the race" and using violence to achieve their ends.

Much of this drama played out in twentieth-century Germany. Emerging from the ashes of World War I, the Weimar Republic— informally named after the city of Goethe and Schiller, the symbol of the German Enlightenment—could not contain the conflict between the radical Left and the radical Right, eventually succumbing to the totalitarianism of the latter. German high culture, so influenced by *Aufklärung* philosophers and writers, found itself dragooned into the service of a regime that turned mass death into an art form and ended in the Götterdämmerung of a bunker beneath Berlin in 1945.

Not far from that bunker, sixty-six years after the capital's fall to the other great totalitarianism of the twentieth century, a German pope speaking in the German parliament called upon an audience of believers and nonbelievers to break out of the mental bunker from which faith is excluded and where reason, cut off from religious truth, withers. And he did so by appealing to knowledge revealed by both faith and reason.

Back to Athens, Rome, and Jerusalem

Pope Benedict XVI asked the assembled legislators this question: What virtue should those in political life cultivate above all? The answer was not empathy, tolerance, or respect for diversity. Instead, he turned to the Hebrew scriptures, specifically the first book of Kings, in which Solomon asks God for "a listening heart"—that is to say, wisdom—"so that he may govern God's people, and discern between good and evil." [2]

The biblical conception of wisdom is not pragmatism or shrewdness. It is knowing the difference between right and wrong and acting accordingly. Wisdom is also considered a more than human quality. It is a *divine* gift: "The Lord gives wisdom" (Proverbs 2:6). For the Jews, wisdom was a deep understanding and was associated with *justice*—hence, its strong identification with the Mosaic law and keeping God's commandments (Ecclesiasticus 1:26–28). Israel's prophets and lawgivers stressed that man's wisdom, enhanced by reflection on history (Deuteronomy 32:7) and observation of the natural world (Proverbs 6:6), is part of his nature, which God gave him, and is not shared by any other earthly creature (Job 35:11).

St. Paul likewise distinguished purely human knowledge from God's wisdom (1 Corinthians 1:17–31). This distinction, Benedict noted, is one reason that Christianity does not propose a political order immediately derived from revelation. Wisdom, for Christians, cannot be reduced to political or judicial rules.

Benedict also observed, however, that Christianity does regard human nature and reason as "true sources of law," coming close to the idea of "natural law developed by the Stoic philosophers," whose broad conception of the *Logos* had come "into contact with leading teachers of Roman Law." [3] Here was a way for all people to understand how to act wisely and justly.

An acknowledgment of these universal moral truths, knowable through reason by believers and nonbelievers alike, is especially important, Benedict informed his listeners, if politics and law are not to degenerate into barbarism. He cited Augustine's famous line, "Without justice—what else is the State but a great band of robbers?" That, the pope pointedly added, was a lesson that the German people had to offer the world in the wake of the Nazi catastrophe.

Continuing his pivot from Jewish, Greek, Roman, and Christian sources to modern times, Benedict stressed that the connection between natural law and justice was understood by many Enlightenment thinkers and is reflected in the Universal Declaration of Human Rights of 1948. Produced partly in reaction to the horrors unleashed by National Socialism, this text was composed by a committee that included a secular French Jew, René Cassin, and a Lebanese Greek Orthodox diplomat and theologian, Charles Malik.

The expression "natural law" appears nowhere in the Universal Declaration, and some of its articles sound more like mid-twentieth-century social democracy than Cicero or Aquinas. But the text's reference to the "inherent dignity and . . . the equal and inalienable rights of all members of the human family" and its assertion that all human beings are "born free and equal in dignity and rights" and "endowed with reason and conscience" borrow the language of natural law, even if they give it an Enlightenment accent.[4] Moreover, the Declaration's composition and endorsement by believers and nonbelievers demonstrates that some principles can be recognized by all men as true.

But this confidence in reason's ability to know truth, Benedict went on, is now in question. The second half of the twentieth century had seen the triumph of "a positivist understanding of nature" throughout the West. By "positivist," the pope meant the idea that reason can know only scientific and social facts and must leave philosophy and religion to the realm of the subjective. Subsequently cut off from "the classical sources of knowledge for ethics and law," the West was trapped in what Benedict described as "a concrete bunker with no windows, in which we ourselves provide lighting and atmospheric conditions, being no longer willing to obtain either from God's wide world." The time had come, said Benedict, for the West to escape this self-imposed prison. "How do we find our way out into the wide world, into the big picture? How can reason rediscover its true greatness, without being sidetracked into irrationality?"

Benedict began his answer by noting that legal positivism's foremost proponent, the Austrian scholar Hans Kelsen (1881–1973), conceded toward the end of his life that the positivist distinction between social fact and human nature was unsustainable. Kelsen was no longer willing to reduce human nature to what he had previously called, using words that reflected a type of scientism, "an aggregate of objective data linked together in terms of cause and effect."

Yet having made this concession, Kelsen hesitated. *If* moral principles were built into human reason, Kelsen reasoned, it could only be because "a will had put them there." But Kelsen maintained that this would, as Benedict put it, "presuppose a Creator God, whose will had entered into [human] nature." For Kelsen, this was a step too far. In his words, "Any attempt to discuss the truth of this belief is utterly futile." [5] Here we come to the nub of the matter. Reflecting on this declaration of futility, Benedict commented, "'Is it really?' I find myself asking. Is it really pointless to wonder whether the objective reason that manifests itself in nature does not presuppose a creative reason, a *Creator Spiritus*?" [6]

A great deal turns not only on the answer to that question but on whether enough people in the West are even willing to consider it. Benedict maintained that without "rational insights" like the reasonable conclusion that there *is* an intelligent Creator, it is hard to imagine how the West could have arrived at "the idea of human rights, the idea of the equality of all people before the law, the recognition of the inviolability of human dignity in every single person and the awareness of people's responsibility for their actions."

More than one Enlightenment

Contemplation of these matters by those who might be regarded as the Enlightenment's present-day representatives is essential for healing the rupture between reason and faith that has left the West vulnerable to pathologies of reason and faith. That contemplation must include a wider and explicit recognition of how particular Enlightenment strands of thought contributed to the emergence of destructive forces such as Marxism and scientism.

But we also need a frank acknowledgment from religious believers that faith in the West has sometimes decoupled itself from natural reason and that Enlightenment thinkers have provided helpful correctives to such developments. At a minimum, believing Jews and Christians should be willing to engage with anyone who thinks there is truth that is more than empirical, not least because such people are plainly seeking a way out of the bunker.

More broadly, we need to ask ourselves: What can we learn today from those instances in which the claims of Enlightenment-influenced reason *have* coexisted peacefully with the claims of the West's two faiths? Finding such examples isn't easy, and we should not expect something approximating perfection. The Jewish and Christian insistence that there is no heaven on earth is an important correction to Enlightenment dreams of perfectibility through science, but it is also a correction to *religious* dreams of a paradise in this world.

Benedict XVI affirmed a crucial distinction between the two great revolutions of the Enlightenment, the French and the American, and before becoming pope he had argued that the latter proved more open to Christianity's integration of reason and faith. He described "the Anglo-Saxon trend, which is more inclined to natural law and tends towards constitutional democracy," as superior to the project associated with Rousseau, which "ultimately aims at complete freedom from any rule." [7]

Recent studies of the political theory underlying the American Founding support Benedict's thesis about the American Revolution. Thomas G. West, for instance, has shown that an emphasis on natural rights was the most consistent link between the political writings of the Founding Fathers, key documents like the Declaration of Independence, and numerous state constitutions and legislation of the time. But West has also shown that these rights were seen as derived from and limited by the natural law. [8]

Others have demonstrated that virtually every American college of the Founding period instructed its students in natural law, emphasizing the connection between natural reason and biblical revelation and how this connection should inform private and public conduct. [9] Against such a background, it is no surprise that the clergyman Moses Hemmenway, a Harvard graduate and a regular correspondent with John Adams, should remind Governor John Hancock and the legislators of Massachusetts in a 1784 sermon that "Natural Liberty does not consist in an exemption from the obligations of morality and the duties of truth, righteousness and kindness to our fellow men.... Our natural rights are bounded and determined by the law of nature." [10]

The French Revolution, which exposed many of the disparities between the Christian ideals of freedom and equality and such premodern customs as hereditary legal privileges, was greeted with jubilation by the champions of Enlightenment reason in Europe and the Americas. But the same revolution resulted in massacres of Christians, of men and women associated with the ancien régime, and eventually of many of the revolutionaries themselves. It spawned political turmoil, economic chaos, and global wars that didn't end until 1815. The triumph of enlightened rationality, it seemed, had unleashed the darkest powers of unreason.

This turn of events plunged many an intellectual into despair. When Napoleon was elected emperor of the French in 1804, Ludwig van Beethoven furiously exclaimed, "Now, too, he will tread under foot all the rights of Man, indulge only his ambition; now he will think himself superior to all men, become a tyrant!" [11] In response to Napoleon's betrayal, Beethoven changed the title of his third symphony from the *Bonaparte* to *Sinfonia eroica, composta per festeggiare il sovvenire di un grand' uomo* ("Heroic Symphony, Composed to Celebrate the Memory of a Great Man").

Across the Atlantic, a different story unfolded, although it has been obscured by the tendency of twentieth-century historians of the American Revolution to give disproportionate attention to the views of such protagonists as Thomas Jefferson, Benjamin Franklin, and Thomas Paine, men who were deeply influenced by the Enlightenment and who rejected central Christian beliefs.

Paine is best known for his immensely influential pamphlet *Common Sense*, published in 1776, which moved opinion in much of colonial America toward the repudiation of British rule and a more egalitarian view of society. Less well known is Paine's book *The Age of Reason: Being an Investigation of True and Fabulous Theology*. Published in three parts beginning in 1794, this text identified organized Christianity as one of the greatest of all despotisms.

Not an atheist, Paine believed that Deism was the only reasonable religious position for enlightened people. He knew that many Americans saw their new regime as the political expression of Enlightenment principles of liberty and reason. Playing to this audience, Paine argued that "a revolution in the system of government" needed to be followed by "a revolution in the system of religion." [12]

Christianity, Paine argued, was a mythology that men whose minds were unfettered by "human inventions and priestcraft" ought to repudiate.[13] "My own mind is my own church," he modestly proclaimed, dismissing the supposed divine revelation and miracles related in the Bible as the hearsay of witnesses who were not to be trusted.[14]

The Age of Reason's influence upon American intellectual and popular opinion was initially substantial. It sold widely, was republished multiple times in the last decade of the eighteenth century, and inspired a slew of publications against organized religion.[15] But Paine's tract also appeared just as the Second Great Awakening, a Protestant evangelical revival, was starting to sweep through the republic.[16] It rendered early-nineteenth-century American society, in the words of the historian Gordon Wood, "much more religious than it had been in the final decades of the eighteenth century." [17]

This religious revival was not confined to the masses. The transformation of a man like the Virginia planter and future congressman, senator, and U.S. minister to Russia, John Randolph of Roanoke, from a flirter with Deism to a fervent evangelical was by no means uncommon.[18]

Though rejecting skepticism and Deism, the evangelical faith embraced by so many Americans neither denounced science nor abandoned the revolution's Enlightenment rhetoric. Instead, it left America with what has been called "the voluntary establishment of religion" [19] and dissociated the word "enlightened" from the philosophical skepticism and hostility to revealed religion that persisted in Europe.[20]

Lessons from a New World

One reason that enthusiasm for Paine's anti-Christian polemic was short-lived was that many Americans came to associate it with the French Revolution's all-out assault on Christianity, which profoundly disturbed influential American Founders. The persecution of Christians by French revolutionaries was a major influence on Alexander Hamilton's return to the deep Christian faith of his youth.[21] As one historian writes, the French Revolution confirmed some Americans' suspicion "that religious skepticism led straight to social and political chaos."[22]

Looking beyond the immediate context, Paine and those who thought as he did failed to recognize two related characteristics of American society. The first was the ongoing permeation of the American colonies during the Age of Reason by organized religion, specifically Protestant Christianity. As Caroline Winterer writes in her study of the Enlightenment in North America, "Of all the institutions organizing American public and private life during the eighteenth century, religion was by far the most important."[23] Religious observances gave structure to people's daily lives. Theological tracts, homilies, and confessional statements constituted the most numerous printed materials.[24]

Some Americans favored removing the established status of particular confessions in particular colonies—for example, the privileges enjoyed in Virginia by the Anglican Church, against which Jefferson railed. But opposition to religious establishments was not the same as hostility to the Christian faith per se. In 1802, Samuel Adams, a revolutionary firebrand and devout Congregationalist, furiously rebuked his friend Paine for what he saw as his effort to de-Christianize America.[25]

The second characteristic of American society that Paine and like-minded observers did not appreciate was the deep familiarity of educated religious opinion in pre- and post-Revolutionary America with Enlightenment thought, especially that emanating from what has been called "the Protestant international"—Northern Germany, Scandinavia, the Netherlands, England, and Scotland.

Presbyterian ministers were especially influential in eighteenth-century American educational institutions. Through their work, the ideas of people like Francis Hutcheson and Thomas Reid—Christians who simultaneously engaged, promoted, and critiqued Enlightenment ideas—influenced many Founders and thus left a mark upon American political culture.[26] John Witherspoon frankly affirmed, "Philosophy, because it is an inquiry into the nature and grounds of moral obligation by reason, [is] distinct from revelation."[27] But he also held that "the discoveries of reason cannot be contrary" to the scriptures and insisted that "there is nothing certain or valuable in moral philosophy, but what is perfectly coincident with Scripture."[28] Likewise William Smith, the Anglican minister appointed provost of the College of Philadelphia in 1755 at the behest of Benjamin Franklin, expounded an educational philosophy that emphasized that the tenets of Christianity could be verified by natural reason.[29]

Nor did these Americans necessarily associate the intellectual tools of the Enlightenment, such as empirical reasoning, with atheist *philosophes*. The primary exponents of this mode of inquiry were in fact clergymen, who incorporated it into religious instruction in American towns and villages.

Many men of the cloth, practicing the scientific method and using instruments imported from Europe, accumulated a considerable amount of empirical information about the workings of the natural world. Few of them, however, lost their sense that a creative God was ultimately in charge and that he designed and continued to shape the world. In *The Christian Philosopher* (1721), the New England Puritan minister Cotton Mather combined the empirical study of fossils with theological reflection, concluding that the empirical sciences and philosophy were "no Enemy, but a mighty and wondrous Incentive to Religion." [30]

At the end of the eighteenth century, identical sentiments could be found in the poem "Greenfield Hill," composed in 1794 by Timothy Dwight IV, a Congregational theologian, the founder of the Connecticut Academy of Arts and Sciences, and the eighth president of Yale College. Rebuking Voltaire and Hume, Dwight speaks of an America in which "Full-rising Science" will cast "unclouded light" and deep harmony between the "proofs of Reason, and the voice of HEAVEN" will prevail. Above all, "Greenfield Hill" expresses Dwight's confidence that the future America would reflect

> One scheme of science, and of morals one;
> And God's own Word the structure, and the base,
> One faith extend, one worship, and one praise. [31]

A prominent defender of orthodox religion and a conspicuous critic of Thomas Paine, Dwight was an important figure in the Second Great Awakening and took a sober view of the tendency of the late continental Enlightenment to emphasize reason over revelation, especially after the French Revolution. But as these words and his own career as a man deeply interested in the natural sciences indicate, Dwight did not reject what he and other ministers saw as the achievements of the Enlightenment—all of which were, to his mind, ultimately derived from the "Word."

Enlightenment, revelation, Logos

Among the men who severed the American colonies' political ties with Britain in 1776 were the Epicurean Deist Thomas Jefferson, the Presbyterian minister John Witherspoon, and the Catholic Charles

Carroll. Neither Witherspoon nor Carroll endorsed Jefferson's religious ideas or his occasional outbursts against Christianity. Despite their religious differences with Jefferson, however, neither the Presbyterian nor the Catholic hesitated to sign the Declaration of Independence drafted by Jefferson. They evidently found nothing in the text incompatible with their religious convictions.

As Gordon Wood writes, "For all their talk of reason and enlightenment, Washington and the other leading Founders were more religious than they sometimes seem." [32] Consider, for example, Washington's letter of farewell to the army, written in June 1783, in which he identifies the three sets of ideas on which the new republic has been built:

> The foundation of our Empire was not laid in the gloomy age of Ignorance and Superstition, but at an Epocha [*sic*] when the rights of mankind were better understood and more clearly defined, than at any former period, the researches of the human mind, after social happiness, have been carried to a great extent, the Treasures of knowledge, acquired by the labors of Philosophers, Sages and Legislatures, through a long succession of years, are laid open for our use, and their collected wisdom may be happily applied in the Establishment of our forms of Government; the free cultivation of Letters, the unbounded extension of Commerce, the progressive refinement of Manners, the growing liberality of sentiment, and above all, the pure and benign light of Revelation, have had ameliorating influence on mankind and increased the blessings of Society. [33]

Washington points first to the classical heritage, the "Philosophers, Sages and Legislatures" of Greece and Rome to whom he and the other Founders looked for guidance. Jefferson, writing to Henry Lee in 1825, identified Aristotle and Cicero as two sources for the emphasis in the Declaration of Independence on the pursuit of human happiness.[34] Many Founders studied classical rhetoric and Roman law and consciously modeled themselves on Greco-Roman statesmen.

After invoking the authority of classical antiquity, Washington cites the "rights of mankind," "the free cultivation of Letters," "the unbounded extension of Commerce," "the progressive refinement of Manners," and the "growing liberality of sentiment"—language that speaks of the Enlightenment, but with a British accent, not that of late-eighteenth century France. Rousseau's disdain for commerce is a matter of record, while Voltaire's satirical polemics flouted good manners. Nor do Washington's words reflect any sympathy for continental admirers of enlightened absolutism.

More important than these classical and Enlightenment sources, however, is the authority that Washington honors "above all"—"the pure and benign light of Revelation." Much ink has been spilled trying to define Washington's precise theological beliefs. Some regard his religious habits and language as typical of the Virginia Anglicans of his time. Others see him as somewhat Deistic.[35] But while Washington sometimes sounded like a Deist, he also believed in the efficacy of prayer.[36] That's not a Deistic position, and his invocation of "the pure and benign light of Revelation," which in the context is clearly a reference to the Jewish and Christian scriptures, points beyond the detached clockmaker of some Deists.

In their book *Washington's God*, Michael Novak and Jana Novak observe that the God who most often comes to mind when reading Washington's statements about religion is the God of the Hebrew prophets, a Being whose ways may be inscrutable and mysterious but who is at work in human history.[37] He "alone," as Washington reminded Benedict Arnold in 1775, "is the Judge of Men's Hearts." [38]

Washington's general appeal to revelation allowed him to transcend the confessional divisions among Protestants in an overwhelm-
ingly Protestant nation and also embrace two religious minorities
then widely distrusted. In letters written to Jews and Catholics in
1790, Washington included phrases that echoed the references to the
Enlightenment and the Bible in his farewell letter to the army: "father
of all mercies," "Divine Providence," "natural rights," "liberal policy,"
"liberality," "the cultivation of manners, morals and piety," "free government," and "good government." [39]

The oratory of the American Founding was saturated with the
language of the Enlightenment, but Washington invoked the Divinity by a decidedly pre-Enlightenment name in his letter of 1789 to
the Hebrew Congregation of Savannah:

> May the same wonder-working Deity, who long since deliv-
> ering the Hebrews from their Egyptian Oppressors planted
> them in the promised land—whose providential agency has
> lately been conspicuous in establishing these United States
> as an independent nation—still continue to water them
> with the dews of Heaven and to make the inhabitants of
> every denomination participate in the temporal and spiri-
> tual blessings of that people whose God is *Jehovah*.[40]

Lest Washington's biblical nomenclature be considered unrep-
resentative, Michael Novak reminds us that the words of "Biblical
metaphysics" and "the Jewish Vision of the world outlined in the
New Testament" permeate the writings of most Founders.[41] In a
study of the comparative influence of different European sources on
late-eighteenth-century American political thought, Donald Lutz
calculates that of the approximately 3,154 citations in political writings by prominent Americans published between 1760 and 1805,

some 34 percent—by far the most—are biblical, the scriptural text most cited being the book of Deuteronomy.[42]

We also find judicious mixtures of Enlightenment and religious motifs in the writings of Alexander Hamilton, who argued in his essay *The Farmer Refuted*, "The sacred rights of mankind are not to be rummaged for among old parchments or musty records. They are written, as with a sunbeam, in the whole volume of human nature, by the hand of the divinity itself, and can never be erased or obscured by mortal power."[43]

"Sunbeam" is evocative of the Enlightenment. So too are the words "the whole volume of human nature." The attachment of the word "sacred" to "rights," however, implies something holy, beyond mortal men. Hamilton's use of the verb "written" implies choice and action by an active divinity whose hand imprints moral norms in human nature itself and is reminiscent of Paul's reference to the universal law written on all human hearts (Romans 2:15).

Other American Founders were even more explicit in connecting the Enlightenment's language of freedom with the God of the Bible. "Our liberties," proclaimed the deeply religious John Dickinson in 1776, "do not come from charters; for these are only the declaration of preexisting rights. They do not depend on parchments or seals; but come from the King of Kings and the Lord of all the Earth."[44]

Decline is not inevitable

By 1792, few French revolutionaries were borrowing phrases from scripture. Few had ever been inclined to do so. But biblical metaphysics and language continued to present no great difficulty for America's Founders. Dickinson's words were even quoted 221 years later by none other than the head of the Catholic Church as John Paul II accepted the credentials of an American ambassador to the Holy See.[45]

That is not to say that the French Revolution lacked American supporters. Within four years of the ratification of the U.S. Constitution in 1788, differing attitudes toward the French Revolution opened a major political cleavage in the still-fragile republic. Jefferson viewed the upheaval in France as a step toward what he would later celebrate as the reign of the "unbounded exercise of reason," which would banish the slavery of "monkish ignorance and superstition." [46]

Jefferson's barbed reference to Christianity is a reminder that traditional religion and Enlightenment secularism have clashed at times in America. Today some secularists would expunge religious reference points from American public life, and particular scholars regard the radical privatization of faith as a necessary consequence of America's Enlightenment roots.[47]

Some of the ways that the culture and politics of an earlier America integrated reason and faith are not replicable in the twenty-first-century West. We live in very different times. But past successes indicate that a winner-take-all conflict between reason and faith is not inevitable. There is enough—indeed, more than enough—in the thought of Plato, in the reflections of Ben Sira of Jerusalem, in the Gospel of John, and in the works of thinkers from Cicero, Augustine, and Maimonides to Newton, Montesquieu, and Blackstone to shore up the walls of reason and faith against the battering waves of philosophical materialism, liberal religion, Prometheanism, scientism, authoritarian relativism, and jihadism.

Above all, there must be a common commitment to the full-bodied reason that includes but transcends the empirical. But that commitment in turn depends on the recognition that if there is a God—whether we call him First Cause, Yahweh Sabaoth, Jesus of Nazareth, Pantokrator, Divine Providence, or Supreme Being—he must be the *Logos*, whose rationality and liberty are reflected in our reason and in our ability to choose freely to know and live in truth.

Without *Logos*, the West is lost. Decline, however, is not inescapable. The free choice for *Logos*, and thus for reason and faith, is never beyond us. The desire for truth, liberty and justice is simply part of who we are. To give rational form to these human longings is thus to act in a way which is truly enlightening, fully consonant with the faiths of the West, and to build a future grounded on the sure knowledge that it is the truth which sets us free.

Notes

Chapter One: The Speech That Shook the World

1. The full text of this dialogue may be found at Manuel Paleologus, *Dialogues with a Learned Moslem*, accessed October 11, 2017, http://www.tertullian.org/fathers/manuel_paleologus_dialogue7_trans.htm.

2. See *John Barker, Manuel II Palaeologus (1391–1425): A Study in Late Byzantine Statesmanship* (New Brunswick, N.J.: Rutgers University Press, 1969).

3. Benedict XVI, "Faith, Reason and the University: Memories and Reflections, September 12, 2006," accessed September 11, 2017, https://w2.vatican.va/content/benedict-xvi/en/speeches/2006/september/documents/hf_ben-xvi_spe_20060912_university-regensburg.html.

4. Benedict XVI, "Faith, Reason and the University."

5. By "Islamism" or "Islamist," I follow the definition offered by Emin Poljarevic, "Islamism," in *The Oxford Encyclopedia of Islam and Politics*, Oxford Islamic Studies Online, accessed April 10, 2018, http://0-www.oxfordislamicstudies.com.mylibrary.qu.edu.qa/article/opr/t342/e0252). "The term 'Islamism' at the very least represents a form of social and political activism, grounded in an idea that public and political life should be guided by a set of Islamic principles. In other words, Islamists are those who believe that Islam has an important role to play in organizing a Muslim-majority society and who seek to implement this belief."

6. Jean Lacouture, *De Gaulle: The Rebel 1890–1944* (New York: Norton, 1990), 166.

7. Winston Churchill, "Their Finest Hour, Speech to the House of Commons, 18 June, 1940," accessed January 24, 2018, https://winstonchurchill.org/resources/speeches/1940-the-finest-hour/their-finest-hour/.

8. See Lynn Hunt, Thomas R. Martin, Barbara H. Rosenwein, R. Po-chia Hsia and Bonnie G. Smith, *The Making of the West: Peoples and Cultures* (Boston: Bedford/St. Martin's, 2009), 712–13.

9. Michael Provence, *The Last Ottoman Generation and the Making of the Modern Middle East* (Cambridge: Cambridge University Press, 2017), 13–14.

10. Lord Acton, "History of Freedom in Antiquity, An Address Delivered to the Members of the Bridgnorth Institute, 26 February 1877," accessed September 13, 2017, https://acton.org/research/history-freedom-antiquity.
11. Karl Marx and Friedrich Engels, *Works*, vol. 3 (London: Penguin, 1971), 33.
12. See Arrian, *The Campaigns of Alexander*, trans. Aubrey de Sélincourt (London: Penguin Classics, 1975), 201–255.
13. On this subject, see Servais Pinckaers, O.P., *The Sources of Christian Ethics* (Washington, D.C.: Catholic University Press, 1995).
14. Edward Gibbon, *The Decline and Fall of the Roman Empire*, ed. J. B. Bury (New York: Fred de Fau and Co., 1906), vol. I, chap. III (1776), accessed October 21, 2017, http://oll.libertyfund.org/titles/gibbon-the-history-of-the-decline-and-fall-of-the-roman-empire-vol-1.
15. Thomas C. Leonard, *Illiberal Reformers: Race, Eugenics, & American Economics in the Progressive Era* (Princeton, NJ: Princeton University Press, 2016), 110.
16. Thomas C. Leonard, *Illiberal Reformers*, 98.
17. Cited in ibid., 110.
18. Ibid., 121.
19. Woodrow Wilson, *A History of the American People* (New York: Harper and Brothers, 1918), vol. 10, 98.
20. Leonard, *Illiberal Reformers*, 160.
21. Ibid., 185.
22. See ibid, 176, 185.
23. See Joseph Ratzinger, *Truth and Tolerance* (San Francisco: Ignatius Press, 2004), 138.
24. See ibid.
25. Friedrich Schleiermacher, *Über die Religion: Reden an die Gebildeten unter ihrer Verächtern*, Philosophische Bibliothek, vol. 225 (Hamburg: F. Meiner, 1799/1958), 30.
26. Ratzinger, *Truth and Tolerance*, 139.
27. Ibid.
28. Ibid., 143.
29. Ibid.
30. Ibid., 142.
31. See Jean Daniélou, S.J., *Essai sur le mystère de l'histoire* (Paris: Editions du Seuil, 1953), 120.
32. Benedict XVI, "It Was a Splendid Day, Benedict XVI Recalls," *L'Osservatore Romano*, October 11, 2012, http://www.osservatoreromano.va/en/news/it-was-a-splendid-day-benedict-xvi-recalls.

Chapter Two: Making the West

1. Gibbon, *Decline and Fall of the Roman Empire*, vol. 6, chap. XXXVIII (1788–1789), accessed November 2, 2017, http://oll.libertyfund.org/titles/gibbon-the-history-of-the-decline-and-fall-of-the-roman-empire-vol-6.
2. Ibid.
3. Ibid.

4. See Louis Feldman, "Palestinian and Diaspora Judaism in the First Century," in *Christianity and Rabbinic Judaism: A Parallel History of their Origins and Early Development*, Hershel Shanks, ed. (Washington: Biblical Archaeology Society, 2011), 6–7.

5. Gibbon, *Decline and Fall of the Roman Empire*, vol. 2, chap. XV (1781), accessed November 2, 2017, http://oll.libertyfund.org/titles/gibbon-the-history-of-the-decline-and-fall-of-the-roman-empire-vol-2.

6. Ibid.

7. Ibid.

8. Claude Tresmontant, *The Origins of Christian Philosophy*, trans. Mark Pontifex (New York: Hawthorn Books, 1963), 61.

9. Ibid., 31.

10. Ibid., 17–18.

11. John Finnis, "Rupture, Transformation and Continuity in the Tradition of Reason and Justice," Charla Magistral: Inauguración del año académico 2013 de la Facultad de Derecho, Pontificia Universidad Católica Argentina, Lunes 22 de Abril de 2013, 32.

12. Tresmontant, *Origins of Christian Philosophy*, 33.

13. See Werner Heisenberg, *The Physicist's Conception of Nature* (New York: Harcourt Brace, 1958).

14. Thorleif Boman, *Hebrew Thought Compared with Greek* (New York: Norton, 1960), 67.

15. Ibid., 69.

16. See, for example, D. J. Furley, "Aristotle on the Voluntary," *Articles on Aristotle*, vol. 2, *Ethics and Politics*, Jonathan Barnes, Malcolm Schofield, and Richard Sorabji, eds. (New York: St. Martin's Press, 1978), 47–60.

17. See Richard Bett, *Pyrrho, His Antecedents, and His Legacy* (Oxford: Clarendon Press, 2000).

18. See J. Dillon, *The Heirs of Plato. A Study of the Old Academy, 347–274 B.C.* (Oxford: Clarendon Press, 2003).

19. See Cyril Bailey, *The Greek Atomists and Epicurus* (Oxford: Clarendon Press, 1928).

20. See C. C. W. Taylor, *The Atomists: Leucippus and Democritus. Fragments, A Text and Translation with Commentary* (Toronto: University of Toronto Press, 1999).

21. See N. T. Wright, *Paul: A Biography* (New York: HarperOne, 2018), 3–4.

22. See Mark L. McPherran, *The Religion of Socrates* (University Park: Pennsylvania State University Press, 1999).

23. See Mor Segev, *Aristotle on Religion* (Cambridge: Cambridge University Press, 2017), 130–39.

24. Aristotle, *Metaphysics* 12.1072b, accessed October 16, 2017, http://www.perseus.tufts.edu/hopper/text?doc=Perseus:abo:tlg,0086,025:12:1072b.

25. Christopher Shields, *Aristotle* (New York: Taylor & Francis, 2007), 222.

26. See E. Mary Smallwood, "The Diaspora in the Roman period before C.E. 70," *The Cambridge History of Judaism*, vol. 3, *The Early Roman Period*, William Horbury,

W. D. Davies, and John Sturdy, eds. (Cambridge: Cambridge University Press, 1984), 168–91.

27. See Salo W. Baron, *A Social and Religious History of the Jews* (New York: Columbia University Press, 1952), vol. 1, 170, 370–72.

28. See J. Andrew Overman, "The God-Fearers: Some Neglected Features," *Journal for the Study of the New Testament* 10, no. 32 (1988): 17–26.

29. See Feldman, "Palestinian and Diaspora Judaism in the First Century," 21–25.

30. See Maren Niehoff, *Philo of Alexandria: An Intellectual Biography* (New Haven: Yale University Press, 2018).

31. See Marian Hillar, "Philo of Alexandria (c. 20 B.C.E.–40 C.E.)," *Internet Encyclopedia of Philosophy*, accessed October 10, 2017, http://www.iep.utm.edu/philo/#H9.

32. See Philo Judaeus, "Quod deus sit immutabilis," *Philonis Alexandrini opera quae supersunt* (Berlin: Reimer, 1897, repr. De Gruyter, 1962), vol. 2, 56–94.

33. See Boman, *Hebrew Thought Compared with Greek*, 65.

34. Ibid., 60.

35. Ibid.

36. See ibid., 69.

37. See Feldman, "Palestinian and Diaspora Judaism in the First Century," 6–8, 21, 34–39.

38. See Jerry L. Daniels, "Anti-Semitism in the Hellenistic-Roman Period," *Journal of Biblical Literature*, 98, no. 1 (1979), 45–65.

39. See Feldman, "Palestinian and Diaspora Judaism in the First Century," 28.

40. Marcus Minucius Felix, *The Octavius of Minucius Felix*, chap. VI, accessed October 12, 2017, http://www.tertullian.org/fathers2/ANF-04/anf04-34.htm.

41. See Wright, *Paul*, 217.

42. Abraham Heschel, *Les Batisseurs du temps* (Paris: Éditions de Minuit, 1957), 27.

43. See John Finnis, *Moral Absolutes: Tradition, Revision, and Truth* (Washington: Catholic University of America Press, 1991), 9–10.

44. See Justin Martyr, *First Apology*, chap. 59, accessed October 15, 2017, http://www.newadvent.org/fathers/0126.htm.

45. See Justin Martyr, *First Apology*, chap. 5, accessed October 15, 2017, http://www.newadvent.org/fathers/0126.htm.

46. Clement of Alexandria, *Stromata* I, 18, 90, 1, accessed October 18, 2017, http://www.newadvent.org/fathers/02101.htm.

47. See Clement of Alexandria, *Exhortation to the Heathens*, chaps. 5, 6, 7, and 11, accessed November 21, 2017, http://www.newadvent.org/fathers/0208.htm.

48. See George Hourani, *Reason and Tradition in Islamic Ethics* (Cambridge: Cambridge University Press, 1985).

49. See Josef Van Ess, *Une lecture à rebours de l'histoire du Mu'tazilisme* (Paris: Geuthner, 1984).

50. T. Gilby, O.P., ed., *St. Thomas Aquinas, Summa Theologiae* (London: Blackfriars, 1963), I, q.2, a.3.

51. Benedict XVI, "Meeting with Representatives from the World of Culture, Collège des Bernardins, Paris, September 12, 2008," accessed December 2, 2017, https://w2.vatican.va/content/benedict-xvi/en/speeches/2008/september/documents/hf_ben-xvi_spe_20080912_parigi-cultura.html.

52. See Frederick Copleston, S.J., *A History of Philosophy*, Bk. 1, vol. IIII, *Ockham to Suárez* (New York: Image Books, 1985), 153–67.

53. See ibid., 161–67.

54. See Bernard R. Goldstein, *The Astronomy of Levi ben Gerson (1288–1344)* (New York: Springer-Verlag, 1985).

55. See P. C. Solon, "The six wings of Immanuel Bonfils and Michael Chrysokokkes," *Centaurus* 15 (1970): 1–20.

56. See Dimitri Gutas, *Greek Thought, Arabic Culture: The Graeco-Arabic Translation Movement in Baghdad and Early Abbāsid Society* (Oxford: Routledge, 1998).

57. See Sylvain Gouguenheim, *Aristote au mont Saint-Michel: les racines grecques de l'Europe chrétienne* (Paris: Éditions du Seuil, 2008).

58. See Copleston, *Ockham to Suárez*, 164–65.

59. See ibid., 167.

60. Benedict XVI, "Meeting with Representatives from the World of Culture."

61. See James Schall, S.J., *On Islam* (San Francisco: Ignatius Press, 2018), 137–38.

Chapter Three: Reason and Its Corruptions

1. See George Gamow, *The Great Physicists from Galileo to Einstein* (Mineola, N.Y.: Dover Publications, 2012), 51.

2. See Rev. 1:8, 4:8, 11:17, 15:3, 16:7, 16:14, 19:6, 19:15, and 21:22.

3. See Peter Byrne, *Natural Religion and the Nature of Religion: The Legacy of Deism* (Milton Park: Routledge, 2013), 52–110.

4. Rob Iliffe, *Priest of Nature: The Religious Worlds of Isaac Newton* (Oxford: Oxford University Press, 2017), 141, 143.

5. Ibid., 4.

6. Ibid., 10–23.

7. Ibid., 4.

8. Isaac Newton, *Sir Isaac Newton's Mathematical Principles of Natural Philosophy and His System of the World*, ed. Florian Cajore (Berkeley: University of California Press, 1960), 79–80.

9. See Pierre Duhem, "Revue de *L'Avenir du Christianisme*," *Revue des questions scientifiques* 55 (1904), 260.

10. Voltaire, *La Henriade*. In *Studies on Voltaire and the Eighteenth Century*, ed. O. R. Taylor (Oxford: Oxford University Press, 1965), vol. 39, 352.

11. Frederick II, "The Political Testament of 1768." In *Die politischen Testamente der Hohenzollern*, ed. Richard Dietrich (Munich: DTV Deutscher Taschenbuch, 1983), 600.

12. Voltaire, "Correspondance avec le roi de Prusse–De Voltaire, Janvier 5, 1767." In *Oeuvres complètes de Voltaire*, ed. George Avenel (Paris: Edition du journal, 1869), vol. 7, 184.

13. Frederick II, "The Political Testament of 1752." In *Die politischen Testamente der Hohenzollern*, ed. Richard Dietrich (Munich: DTV Deutscher Taschenbuch, 1983), 454.

14. See Selma Stern, *Der preussische Staat und die Juden: Die Zeit Friedrichs des Grossen* (Tubingen: Mohr Siebeck 1971), vol 1: Darstellung, 7.

15. See Wright, *Paul*, 204.

16. Edward Gibbon, *Essai sur l'étude de la littérature* (1761), 1. In *The Miscellaneous Works of Edward Gibbon*, ed. John Sheffield (London, 1814), vol. IV, 1.

17. Hugh Trevor-Roper, "Gibbon and the Publication of *The Decline and Fall of the Roman Empire*, 1776–1976," *History and the Enlightenment* (New Haven: Yale University Press, 2010), 152.

18. Francis Bacon, *The Physical and Metaphysical Works*, ed. Joseph Devey (London: Bohn, 1853), 375.

19. Ibid., 383.

20. Ibid., 416.

21. Francis Bacon, *Novum Organum Scientiarum*, ed. Joseph Devey, Bk. 1, CXVII, CXXX, accessed October 24, 2017, http://oll.libertyfund.org/titles/bacon-novum-organum.

22. Francis Bacon, *The Moral and Historical Works of Lord Bacon*, ed. J. Devey (London: Bell & Daldy, 1868), 297.

23. Ibid., 298–99.

24. Edward Arber (ed.), *A Harmony of the Essays etc. of Francis Bacon* (Westminster: Constable, 1895), 346.

25. Bacon, *Novum Organum*, Bk. 1, CXVII.

26. Frederick Copleston S.J., *A History of Philosophy*, Bk. 2, vol. IV, *Descartes to Leibniz* (New York: Image Books, 1985), 9.

27. See Thomas Aquinas, *Summa contra gentiles*, trans. James F. Anderson (New York: Hanover House, 1955-57), bk II, chap. 4.

28. See Philippe Minard, *La fortune du colbertism: état et industrie dans la France des Lumières* (Paris: Fayard, 1998).

29. Adam Smith, *An Inquiry into the Nature and the Causes of the Wealth of Nations*, eds. R.H. Campbell and A.S. Skinner (Indianapolis: Liberty Fund, [1776] 1981), vol. I, 428–504.

30. Ulrich L. Lehner, *The Catholic Enlightenment: The Forgotten History of a Global Movement* (Oxford: Oxford University Press, 2016), 3.

31. Caroline Winterer, *American Enlightenments: Pursuing Happiness in the Age of Reason* (New Haven: Yale University Press, 2016), 42.

32. See Pieter M. Judson, *The Habsburg Empire: A New History* (Cambridge: Belknap Press, 2016), 69–70.

33. R.R. Palmer, *Catholics and Unbelievers in Eighteenth Century France* (Princeton: Princeton University Press, 1939), 18.

34. See ibid., 19.

35. Lehner, *The Catholic Enlightenment*, 7.

36. See Judson, *The Habsburg Empire*, 29.
37. Lehner, *The Catholic Enlightenment*, 22.
38. Ibid., 104–110.
39. See ibid., 110–13, 191.
40. Colin Kidd, "Subscription, the Scottish Enlightenment, and the Moderate Interpretation of History," *Journal of Ecclesiastical History* LV (2004), 503.
41. Hugh Blair, "The Importance of Religious Knowledge to the Happiness of Mankind, 1750." In *Sermons*, vol.1 (London: A. Strahan, 1812), 144
42. William Robertson, "The Situation of the World at the Time of Christ's Appearance, and its Connexions with the Success of His Religion Considered, 1755." In *The Works of William Robertson*, vol. 1 (Edinburgh, 1829), lxxvii–lxxxvi.
43. Thomas Reid, *The Correspondence of Thomas Reid*, ed. Paul Wood (Edinburgh: Edinburgh Press, 2002), 38, 40, 97; Thomas Reid, "Essays on the Active Powers of Man," In *The Works of Thomas Reid*, ed. Sir William Hamilton, 6th ed. (Bristol: Thoemmes Press, [1863] 1994), IV.xi: 636a.
44. Ibid., V.ii: 641b.
45. See Thomas Reid, *Lectures on Natural Theology (1780)*, ed. Elmer Duncan (Washington: University Press of America, 1981), 84.
46. Michah Gottlieb, *Faith and Freedom: Moses Mendelssohn's Theological-Political Thought* (Oxford: Oxford University Press, 2011), 20.
47. See ibid., 29.
48. See Moses Mendelssohn, *Jerusalem, or On Religious Power and Judaism*, trans. Allan Arkush (Hanover, N.H.: University Press of New England, 1983).
49. John Locke, *An Essay Concerning Human Understanding*, ed. Alexander Campbell Fraser (Oxford: Clarendon Press, [1690] 1894), vol. 1, II.i.25.
50. C. A. Helvétius, *De l'Esprit, or Essays on the Mind* (London: Vernor, Hood, and Sharpe, 1810), 184.
51. Stephen Hawking and Leonard Mlodinow, *The Grand Design* (New York: Bantam Books, 2010), 5.
52. Ibid., 87.
53. E. O. Wilson, *Sociobiology: The New Synthesis* (Cambridge: Harvard University Press, 1975), 562.

Chapter Four: Faiths of Destruction

1. See Henri de Lubac, S.J., *The Drama of Atheist Humanism* (San Francisco: Ignatius Press, 1995), 26–41.
2. Karl Marx, *The Difference between the Democritean and Epicurean Philosophy of Nature in General* (1841), accessed November 7, 2017, https://archive.org/stream/Marx_Karl_-_Doctoral_Thesis_-_The_Difference_Between_the_Democritean_and_Epicure/Marx_Karl_-_Doctoral_Thesis_-_The_Difference_Between_the_Democritean_and_Epicurean_Philosophy_of_Nature_djvu.txt.
3. Karl Marx, *Capital* (1867), vol. 1, chap. 1, sec. 4, accessed November 7, 2017, https://www.marxists.org/archive/marx/works/1867-c1/ch01.htm#219.
4. Karl Marx, *On the Jewish Question* (1844), accessed November 7, 2017, https://www.marxists.org/archive/marx/works/1844/jewish-question/.

5. Karl Marx, *A Contribution to the Critique of Hegel's Philosophy of Right* (1844), Introduction, accessed November 7, 2017, https://www.marxists.org/archive/marx/works/1843/critique-hpr/intro.htm.
6. Ibid.
7. Friedrich Engels, *Anti-Dühring: Herr Eugen Dühring's Revolution in Science*, Part I: Philosophy, IX. Morality and Law. Eternal Truths (1877), accessed November 7, 2017, https://www.marxists.org/archive/marx/works/1877/anti-duhring/ch07.htm.
8. Ibid.
9. Ibid.
10. Ibid.
11. Eric Voegelin, "Science, Politics, and Gnosticism." In *The Collected Works of* Eric Voegelin, vol. 5, *Modernity without Restraint*, ed. Manfred Henningsen (Columbia, MO: University of Missouri Press, 2000), 262–86.
12. Friedrich Engels and Karl Marx, *The Holy Family: or Critique of Critical Criticism. Against Bruno Bauer and Company*, trans. Richard Dickson (Moscow: Foreign Languages Publishing House, [1945] 1956), 176.
13. Karl Marx, *A Contribution to the Critique of Political Economy*, ed. Maurice Dobbs (New York: International Publishers, 1970), 168.
14. Karl Marx, *Manifesto of the Communist Party* (1848), chapter 1, accessed November 7, 2017, https://www.marxists.org/archive/marx/works/1848/communist-manifesto/ch01.htm#007.
15. Ibid.
16. See, for example, Marx, *A Contribution to the Critique of Political Economy*, 363.
17. Leon Trotsky, *Literature and Revolution* (1924), chapter 8, accessed November 8, 2017, https://www.marxists.org/archive/trotsky/1924/lit_revo/ch08.htm.
18. Ibid.
19. Ibid.
20. Vladimir Lenin, *Religion* (Alcester: Read Books Ltd., 2007), 5.
21. Frederick Copleston S.J., *A History of Philosophy*, Bk. 3, vol. 7, *Fichte to Nietzsche* (New York: Doubleday Books, 1985), 305.
22. Leon Trotsky, "Speech to the Thirteenth Party Congress on May 26, 1924." In *The Challenge of the Left Opposition: 1923–1925*, ed. Naomi Allen (New York: Pathfinder Press, 1975), 161.
23. Karl Marx, "Suppression of the *Neue Rheinische Zeitung*," *Neue Rheinische Zeitung, Final Issue*, no. 301, May 18, 1849, https://www.marxists.org/archive/marx/works/1849/05/19c.htm.
24. Maurice Cowling, *Mill and Liberalism* (Cambridge: Cambridge University Press, 1963/1990), xlviii.
25. John Stuart Mill, *The Collected Works of John Stuart Mill*, vol. I, *Autobiography and Literary Essays*, eds. John M. Robson and Jack Stillinger (Milton Park: Routledge, 1981), 41.
26. Ibid., 221.
27. John Stuart Mill, "Utility of Religion," in *The Collected Works*, vol. X, *Essays on Ethics, Religion, and Society*, ed. John M. Robson (London: Routledge and Kegan Paul, 1985), 426.

28. John Stuart Mill, "On Liberty," *in The Collected Works of John Stuart Mill*, vol. XVIII, *Essays on Politics and Society Part 1*, ed. John M. Robson (London: Routledge and Kegan Paul, 1977), 255.

29. Mill, "Utility of Religion," 424–25.

30. See Jeremy Bentham, *An Introduction to the Principles of Morals and Legislation*, ed. LK. Lafleur (Oxford: Basil Blackwell, 1948), chap.1, sec.1.

31. John Stuart Mill, "Bentham," in *The Collected Works of John Stuart Mill*, vol. X, *Essays on Ethics, Religion, and Society*, ed. John M. Robson (London: Routledge and Kegan Paul, 1985), 178.

32. John Stuart Mill, *Principles of Political Economy with some of their Applications to Social Philosophy*, ed. William James Ashley (London: Longmans, Green and Co., 1920), 759.

33. Cowling, *Mill and Liberalism*, 38. For a comprehensive study of Mill's liberalism as a form of religion, see Linda C. Raeder, *John Stuart Mill and the Religion of Humanity* (Columbia: University of Missouri Press, 2002).

34. John Stuart Mill, "Inaugural Address Delivered to the University of St. Andrews," in *The Collected Works of John Stuart Mill*, vol. XXI, *Essays on Equality, Law, and Education*, ed. John M. Robson, (London: Routledge and Kegan Paul, 1984), 236.

35. Ibid., 240.

36. Ibid., 248.

37. Mill, "Civilization," in *Essays on Politics and Society Part I*, 119.

38. Ibid., 144.

39. Oscar A. Haac, ed., *The Correspondence of John Stuart Mill and Auguste Comte* (New Brunswick, N.J.: Transaction Publishers, 1995), 227.

40. Ibid., 317.

41. Mill, "On Liberty," 255.

42. Friedrich Nietzsche, *The Gay Science*, trans. Walter Kaufmann (New York: Vintage, 1974), 343.

43. Ibid., 344.

44. See Voegelin, "Science, Politics, and Gnosticism," 53–73.

45. Friedrich Nietzsche, *On the Genealogy of Morals* (Oxford: Oxford University Press, 1996), Part II, 126.

46. Friedrich Nietzsche, *The Complete Works of Friedrich Nietzsche*, vol. 15, *The Will to Power: An attempted transvaluation of all values, Books three and four*, ed. Oscar Levy (Edinburgh and London: T. N. Foulis, 1910), 432.

47. Nietzsche, *On the Genealogy of Morals*, Part II, 64–65.

48. Ibid., 128.

49. Friedrich Nietzsche, *The Antichrist*, trans. Walter Kaufmann (New York: Viking, 1954), 2.

50. See Bernard Lewis, *The Assassins: A Radical Sect of Islam* (Oxford: Oxford University Press, 1967).

51. Nietzsche, *On the Genealogy of Morals*, Part II, 126.

52. Nietzsche, *The Will to Power*, 11.

53. Ibid., 127.

54. Ibid.

55. Ibid., 380.

56. Nietzsche, *The Antichrist*, 18.

Chapter Five: Authoritarian Relativism, Liberal Religion, and Jihadism

1. *Planned Parenthood v. Casey*, 505 U.S. 833 (1992).
2. Joseph Ratzinger, "Homily 'Pro Eligendo Romano Pontifice', April 18, 2005," accessed January 20, 2017, http://www.vatican.va/gpII/documents/homily-pro-eligendo-pontifice_20050418_en.html.
3. Ian Markham, *Truth and the Reality of God: An Essay on Natural Theology* (Edinburgh: T&T Clark, 1998), 115.
4. John Henry Newman, "Biglietto speech, 12 May 1879," accessed December 15, 2017, http://www.newmanreader.org/works/addresses/file2.html.
5. Newman, "Biglietto speech."
6. John Henry Newman, *Apologia Pro Vita Sua*, ed. David J. DeLaura (London: W. W. Norton and Company, 1968), 216.
7. John Henry Newman, "JHM to Mrs. Jemima Newman, 13 March 1829," In *The Letters and Diaries of John Henry Newman*, vol. 2: *Tutor of Oriel, January 1827 to December 1831*, eds. Ian Ker and Thomas Gornall S.J. (Oxford: Oxford University Press, 1979), 130.
8. Newman, "Biglietto Speech."
9. Ibid.
10. Ibid.
11. Ibid.
12. John Henry Newman, "To St. George Jackson Mivart, 9 December 1871." In *The Letters and Diaries of John Henry Newman, vol. 25: The Vatican Council: January 1870 to December 1871*, eds. Charles Stephen Dessain and Thomas Gornall S.J. (Oxford: Oxford University Press, 1973), 446.
13. John Henry Newman, *The Idea of a University* (1852), Discourse 4, accessed December 15, 2017, http://www.newmanreader.org/works/idea/discourse4.html.
14. Newman, "Biglietto speech."
15. Cowling, *Mill and Liberalism*, xxxviii.
16. Karl Rahner S.J., "Hell." In *Encyclopedia of Theology: A Concise 'Sacramentum Mundi'* (London: Burns and Oates, 1973), 603.
17. See John Finnis, "Hell and Hope." In *The Collected Essays of John Finnis, vol. v, Religion and Public Reasons* (Oxford: Oxford University Press, 2011), 373.
18. F. L. Cross and E. A. Livingstone, eds., *Oxford Dictionary of the Christian Church*, 2nd ed. (Oxford: Oxford University Press, 1974).
19. Benedict XVI, "Faith, Reason and the University."
20. Martin Luther, *Schriften, Predigten, Disputationen* 1520/21, vol. 8, *D. Martin Luthers Werke* (Weimar: Hermann Böhlau, 1888), 98–99.
21. See Samuel Gregg, "Faith, Reason, and Order: Thomas More and Natural Law." In *Thomas More: Why Patron of Statesmen?* ed. Travis Curtwright (Lanham, Md.: Lexington Books, 2015), 95–110.
22. Schall, *On Islam*, 7.
23. See David Burrell, *Freedom and Creation in Three Traditions* (Notre Dame, IN: University of Notre Dame Press), 91–93.
24. See Hillel Ofek, "Why the Arabic World turned away from Science," *The New Atlantis* 30 (2011): 8–13.
25. Ibid., 13.

26. See Schall, *On Islam*, 106.
27. See Ofek, "Why the Arabic World turned away from Science," 15.
28. See Ulrich Rudolph, *Al-Maturidi and the Development of Sunni Theology in Samarqand*, trans. Rodrigo Adem (Boston: Brill, 2015).
29. See Robert R. Reilly, *The Closing of the Muslim Mind: How Intellectual Suicide Created the Modern Islamist Crisis* (Wilmington, Dela.: ISI Books, 2010), Introduction.
30. Samir Khalil Samir, S.J., *111 Questions about Islam: A Series of Interviews Conducted by Giorgio Paolucci and Camille Eid* (San Francisco: Ignatius Press, 2002), 91.
31. Ibid., 201.
32. See Eric Barendt, *An Introduction to Constitutional Law* (Oxford: Oxford University Press, 1998), 1–15.
33. See Albert Hourani, *A History of the Arab Peoples* (Cambridge, MA: Harvard University Press, 1991), 265–473.
34. Rémi Brague and Pierre Manent, "Taking Religion Seriously," interview by Jacques de Guillebon, trans. Daniel J. Mahoney, and Paul Seaton, *Library of Law and Liberty*, April 27, 2018, http://www.libertylawsite.org/2018/04/27/taking-religion-seriously-lincorrect-manent-brague-debate-islam-christianity-france/.
35. Samir, *111 Questions about Islam*, 201 fn. 45.
36. See Lukas Wick, *Islamic Theology, Constitutionalism, and the State* (Grand Rapids, Mich.: Acton Institute, 2012).
37. See ibid., 131–76.
38. Cited in Robert R. Reilly, "The Formidable Philosophical Obstacles to Islamic Constitutionalism," *Library of Law and Liberty*, February 1, 2013, http://www.libertylawsite.org/liberty-forum/the-formidable-philosophical-obstacles-to-islamic-constitutionalism/.
39. Robert R. Reilly, "Foreword." In Wick, *Islamic Theology, Constitutionalism, and the State*, iii.
40. Pope Francis, "Interview," Full Text of Pope Francis' In-Flight Press Conference from Poland, July 31, 2016, http://www.ncregister.com/daily-news/full-text-of-pope-francis-in-flight-press-conference-from-poland.
41. Alan B. Krueger and Jitka Maleckova, "Education, Poverty and Terrorism: Is There a Causal Connection?" *Journal of Economic Perspectives* 17, no. 4 (2003): 119.
42. Ibid., 141.
43. Robert Barro, "The Myth That Poverty Breeds Terrorism," *Bloomberg News*, June 10, 2002, https://www.bloomberg.com/news/articles/2002-06-09/the-myth-that-poverty-breeds-terrorism.
44. Samir, *111 Questions about Islam*, 65.
45. Pope Francis, "Interview," interview by Guillaume Goubert and Sébastien Maillard, *La Croix*, May 17, 2015, https://www.la-croix.com/Religion/Pape/INTERVIEW-Pope-Francis-2016-05-17-1200760633.
46. Francis, Apostolic Exhortation *Evangelii gaudium*, November 24, 2013, paragraph 253, http://w2.vatican.va/content/francesco/en/apost_exhortations/documents/papa-francesco_esortazione-ap_20131124_evangelii-gaudium.html.
47. Samir, *111 Questions about Islam*, 65.
48. Ibid., 62.

49. Ibid., 75.
50. Samir Khalil Samir S.J., "Points of *Evangelii gaudium* that require clarification," *L'Espresso*, December 13, 2013, http://chiesa.espresso.repubblica.it/articolo/1350689bdc4. html?eng=y.
51. Ibid.
52. Rémi Brague, "With Courage but without Hatred," *First Things*, July 20, 2016, https://www.firstthings.com/web-exclusives/2016/07/with-courage-but-without-hatred.
53. See, for instance, Mustafa Akyol, *Islam Without Extremes* (New York: W.W. Norton & Company, 2011).
54. See Schall, *On Islam*, 121.
55. See Byran Ward-Perkins, *The Fall of Rome and the End of Civilization* (Oxford: Oxford University Press, 2005).

Chapter Six: A Way Back

1. Benedict XVI, "Address to the Roman Curia, December 22, 2005," accessed January 31, 2018, https://w2.vatican.va/content/benedict-xvi/en/speeches/2005/december/documents/hf_ben_xvi_spe_20051222_roman-curia.html.
2. Vernon L. Smith, *The Evidence of Things Not Seen: Reflections on Faith, Science, and Economics* (Grand Rapids, Mich.: Acton Institute, 2017), 16.
3. Ibid.
4. Ibid., 6.
5. Ibid., 7.
6. Ibid., 15.
7. John Locke, "A Letter Concerning Toleration" (1689), accessed December 21, 2017, http://oll.libertyfund.org/titles/locke-a-letter-concerning-toleration-and-other-writings.
8. See Timothy Samuel Shah, "The Roots of Religious Freedom in Early Christian Thought." In *Christianity and Freedom*, vol. 1, *Historical Perspectives*, eds. Timothy Samuel Shah and Allen D. Hertzke (Cambridge: Cambrdige University Press, 2016), 33–61.
9. The Peace specified that realms had to choose between Catholicism and Lutheranism. All other Christian confessions were still considered heretical.
10. "Final Text: The Declaration on Religious Freedom." In David L. Schindler and Nicholas J. Healy Jr., *Freedom, Truth, and Human Dignity: The Second Vatican Council's Declaration on Religious Freedom. A New Translation, Redaction, and Interpretation of Dignitatis Humanae* (Grand Rapids, Mich.: Eerdmans, 2015), paragraph 2 at 389.
11. "Treaty of Amity and Commerce Between His Majesty the King of Prussia, and the United States of America; September 10, 1785," accessed January 21, 2018, http://avalon.law.yale.edu/18th_century/prus1785.asp.
12. Nikolai Bukharin and Yevgenii Preobrazhensky, *The ABC of Communism* (London: Penguin Books, 1969), Section 13.
13. Ibid., Sections 93, 94, 99.

14. John Paul II, Encyclical Letter *Centesimus annus* (1991), paragraph 32, accessed January 31, 2018, http://www.vatican.va/holy_father/john_paul_ii/encyclicals/documents/hf_jp-ii_enc_01051991_centesimus-annus_en.html.
15. First Vatican Council, *Dei Filius* (1870), Introduction, no.7, accessed January 22, 2018, https://www.ewtn.com/library/councils/v1.htm#4.; chapter 2, no. 1.
16. Ibid., chapter 4, no. 5.
17. Ibid., chapter 4, no. 11–12.
18. Finnis, "Rupture, Transformation and Continuity in the Tradition of Reason and Justice," 12.
19. Ibid., 16.
20. Charles Darwin, *The Autobiography of Charles Darwin, 1809–1882: with original omissions restored*, ed. Nora Barlow (London: Collins [1882] 1982), 92.
21. Ibid.
22. Ibid.
23. See Stanley Jaki, *Darwin's Design* (Port Huron, Mich.: Real View Books, 2006).
24. Christoph Schönborn, "*Fides, Ratio, Scientia*: The Debate about Evolution." In *Creation and Evolution*, compiled by Stephan Otto Horn and Siegfied Wiedenhofer, trans. Michael J. Miller (San Francisco: Ignatius Press, 2007), 91.
25. Albert Einstein, *The World As I See It* (Thousand Oaks, Calif.: Snowball Publishing, 2014), 21.
26. See Rudolf Hoess, *Commandant of Auschwitz: The Autobiography of Rudolf Hoess*, trans. Constantine FitzGibbon (New York: Popular Library, 1961).
27. This point is well developed in Edward Feser, "One Circular Argument," *Claremont Review of Books* 17, no. 4 (2017): 57–58.
28. Plato, *The Republic*, trans. Robin Waterfield (Oxford: Oxford University Press, 2008), 328e–331d.
29. Ibid., 338c.
30. Ibid, 352d.
31. Aristotle, *Nicomachean Ethics*, trans. David Ross and ed. Lesley Brown (Oxford: Oxford University Press, 2009), V.1.1129b12-14.
32. See John R. Kroger, "The Philosophical Foundations of Roman Law: Aristotle, the Stoics, and Roman Theories of Natural Law," *Wisconsin Law Review* (2004): 905–944.
33. See John M. Armstrong, "Epicurean Justice," *Phronesis* 42, no. 3 (1997): 324–34.
34. See Finnis, "Rupture, Transformation and Continuity in the Tradition of Reason and Justice," 52.
35. See Wright, *Paul*, 425.
36. See Eugene Hugh Byrne, "Medicine in the Roman Army," *The Classical Journal* 5, no. 6 (1910): 267–72.
37. James Edward McClellan and Harold Dorn, *Science and Technology in World History: An Introduction* (Baltimore MD: Johns Hopkins University Press, 2006), 90–120.
38. See, for instance, Daniel Hall, "Altar and Table: A phenomenology of the surgeon-priest," *Yale Journal of Biology and Medicine* 81, no.4 (2008): 193–98.
39. Finnis, "Rupture, Transformation and Continuity in the Tradition of Reason and Justice," 60.

40. Benedetto Croce, "We Cannot Help But Call Ourselves Christians." In *My Philosophy and Other Essays on the Moral and Political Problems of Our Times*, ed. R. Kilbansky (London: George Allen & Unwin, 1949), 39.

Chapter Seven: On Earth as in Heaven

1. See Jürgen Habermas, "The European nation-state and the pressures of globalization." In *Global Justice and Transnational Politics*, eds. P. de Grief and C. Cronin (Cambridge, Mass.: MIT Press), 217–34.
2. Benedict XVI, "Visit to the Bundestag: The Listening Heart: Reflections on the Foundations of Law, September 22, 2011," accessed February 1, 2018, https://w2.vatican.va/content/benedict-xvi/en/speeches/2011/september/documents/hf_ben-xvi_spe_20110922_reichstag-berlin.html.
3. Ibid.
4. General Assembly of the United Nations, *Universal Declaration of Human Rights*, December 10, 1948, accessed January 13, 2018, https://web.archive.org/web/20141208080853/http://www.un.org/Overview/rights.html.
5. Benedict XVI, "Visit to the Bundestag," citing W. Waldstein, *Ins Herz geschrieben. Das Naturrecht als Fundament einer menschlichen Gesellschaft* (Augsburg, 2010), 19.
6. Benedict XVI, "Visit to the Bundestag."
7. Ratzinger, *Truth and Tolerance*, 238.
8. See Thomas G. West, *The Political Theory of the American Founding: Natural Rights, Public Policy, and the Moral Conditions of Freedom* (Cambridge: Cambridge University Press, 2017).
9. See, for example, Anna Haddow, *Political Science in American Colleges and Universities, 1636–1900* (New York: Octagon Books, 1969), 45, 54–56.
10. Moses Hemmenway, "A sermon, preached before His Excellency John Hancock, Esq; governor; His Honor Thomas Cushing, Esq; lieutenant-governor; the Honorable the Council, and the Honorable the Senate, and House of Representatives, of the Commonwealth of Massachusetts, May 26, 1784. Being the day of general election," accessed July 11, 2018, https://quod.lib.umich.edu/cgi/t/text/text-idx?c=evans;cc=evans;rgn=main;view=text;idno=N14607.0001.001.
11. Ferdinand Ries, cited in *Beethoven: Letters, Journals and Conversations*, ed. Michael Hamburger (New York: Anchor Books, 1960), 29–30.
12. Thomas Paine, *The Age of Reason: Being an Investigation of True and Fabulous Theology*, ed. Moncure Daniel Conway (New York: Merchant Books [1794] 2010), 5.
13. Ibid., 6.
14. Ibid., 6–8.
15. See Gordon S. Wood, *Empire of Liberty: A History of the Early Republic, 1789–1815* (Oxford: Oxford University Press, 2009), 199–200.
16. Ibid., 582.
17. Ibid., 576.
18. Ibid., 590.
19. See Elwyn A. Smith, "Voluntary Establishment of Religion." In *The Religion of the Republic*, ed. Elwyn A. Smith (Philadelphia: Fortress Press, 1971) 154–82.
20. Winterer, *American Enlightenments*, 252.

21. See Forrest McDonald, *Alexander Hamilton: A Biography* (New York: W.W. Norton & Company, 1979), 356–57.

22. Winterer, *American Enlightenments*, 175.

23. Ibid., 173.

24. See Patricia U. Bonomi, *Under the Cope of Heaven: Religion, Society, and Politics in Colonial America* (Oxford: Oxford University Press, 2003), 3–4.

25. See John Keane, *Tom Paine: A Political Life* (Boston: Bloomsbury, 1995), 475–76.

26. Daniel N. Robertson, "The Scottish Enlightenment and the American Founding," *The Monist* 90, no. 2 (2007): 170–81.

27. John Witherspoon, *Works of the Rev. John Witherspoon*, vol. 3, *Containing Sermons on Doctorial and Practical Subjects for The People of God* (Grand Rapids, Mich.: Reformation Heritage Books, 2000), 367.

28. Ibid., 471.

29. See Gideon Mailer, *John Witherspoon's American Revolution: Enlightenment and Religion from the Creation of Britain to the Founding of the United States* (Chapel Hill: University of North Carolina Press, 2017).

30. Cotton Mather, *The Christian Philosopher*, ed. Winton U. Solberg (Urbana: University of Illinois Press, [1721] 2000), 97.

31. Timothy Dwight, *Greenfield Hill: A Poem in Seven Parts* (New York, 1791), 168.

32. Wood, *Empire of Liberty*, 585.

33. George Washington, "Circular Letter of Farewell to the Army, June 8, 1783," accessed February 1, 2018, http://www.loc.gov/teachers/classroommaterials/ presentationsandactivities/presentations/timeline/amrev/peace/circular.html.

34. "From Thomas Jefferson to Henry Lee, May 8, 1825," accessed February 2, 2018, https://founders.archives.gov/documents/Jefferson/98-01-02-5212.

35. See Michael Novak, *On Two Wings: Humble Faith and Common Sense at the American Founding* (New York: Encounter Books, 2002), 125–76.

36. Wood, *Empire of Liberty*, 585.

37. See Michael Novak and Jana Novak, *Washington's God* (New York: Basic Books, 2006).

38. "From George Washington to Colonel Benedict Arnold, September 14, 1775," accessed February 4, 2018, https://founders.archives.gov/documents/ Washington/03-01-02-0355.

39. See "From George Washington to the Hebrew Congregation in Newport, Rhode Island, August 18, 1790," accessed February 5, 2018, https://founders.archives.gov/ documents/Washington/05-06-02-0135; and "From George Washington to Roman Catholics in America, c.15 March 1790," accessed February 6, 2018, https://founders. archives.gov/documents/Washington/05-05-02-0193.

40. "From George Washington to the Savannah, Ga., Hebrew Congregation, June 14, 1790," accessed February 6, 2018, https://founders.archives.gov/documents/ Washington/05-05-02-0279. Emphasis added.

41. Novak, *On Two Wings*, 7.

42. See Donald S. Lutz, "The Relative Influence of European Writers on Late Eighteenth-Century American Political Thought," *American Political Science Review* 78, no.1 (1984): 189–97. The English jurist William Blackstone and the French philosopher Montesquieu account for 7.9 percent and 8.3 percent each.

Locke and Hume amount to 2.9 percent and 2.7 percent respectively. Locke was the most quoted political writer between 1760 and 1775 in the lead-up to the American Revolution.

43. "The Farmer Refuted, February 23, 1775," accessed February 4, 2018, https://founders.archives.gov/documents/Hamilton/01-01-02-0057.
44. John Dickinson, cited in Novak, *On Two Wings*, 75.
45. See John Paul II, "Address to Her Excellency Mrs. Corinne (Lindy) Claiborne Boggs, New Ambassador of the United States of America to the Holy See, December 16, 1997," accessed January 29, 2018, https://w2.vatican.va/content/john-paul-ii/en/speeches/1997/december/documents/hf_jp-ii_spe_19971216_ambassador-usa.html.
46. "Letter from Thomas Jefferson to Roger C. Weightman, Monticello, June 24, 1826," accessed February 3, 2018, https://www.loc.gov/exhibits/declara/rcwltr.html.
47. See, for instance, Patrick Deneen, *Why Liberalism Failed* (New Haven: Yale University Press, 2018), and Kenneth R. Craycraft Jr., *The American Myth of Religious Freedom* (Dallas: Spence Publishing, 1999).

Index

Paul, Saint, 4, 27, 30, 41–45, 48, 54, 67, 126, 145, 151, 164
Pauli, Wolfgang, 17–18
Peace of Augsburg, 129
Persian Empire, 9
Pelagianism, 106
Philo of Alexandria, 37
Pinckaers, O.P., Servais, 10
Pius IX, Pope, 105, 134
Planck, Max, 17
Planned Parenthood v. Casey, 101
Plato, 4, 6, 10, 29, 32–33, 66, 140–41, 143, 165
Poland, 5, 7
polis, 34, 141
Pontius Pilate, 26, 144
Pope, Alexander, 54
positivism, 49, 152–53
poverty, 3, 19, 118–19, 132
Philosophiae Naturalis Principia Mathematica, 53
Preobrazhensky, Yevgeni, 132
Princeton University, 70
Principles of Political Economy, 91
progress, 13, 16, 48, 57–59, 62, 74, 76, 89, 93, 130
Progressives, 13–15
Prometheanism, 73, 76, 84–85, 87, 100, 122, 165
Prometheus, 73
property, 75, 87, 132, 141
proskynesis, 9
Providence, 55–56, 163, 165
Prussia, 58, 82, 128, 131
public sphere, 74–75
Pyrrho of Elis, 33

R

race science, 13–15,
Rahner S.J., Karl, 109
Randolph of Roanoke, John, 157
Ratzinger, Joseph, xiii–xiv, 2, 16–20, 103. *See also* Benedict XVI (pope)
reason
  deductive, 46
  empirical, 18, 46, 76, 84, 102, 104–105, 108, 135, 138, 154, 159–60
  inductive, 60, 91, 135
  natural, 41, 108, 142, 154–55, 159
  pathologies of, 16, 73, 82, 100, 123, 127, 146, 154
  right, 62,
  scientific, 19, 98
Reasonableness of Christianity, 69
Reformation, the, 11,
Regensburg, town of, 1, 3, 4, 16
Regensburg address, 2–3, 16, 47, 110
Reid, Thomas, 70, 159,
Reilly, Robert, 112, 117
relativism, authoritarian, 5, 103, 106, 110, 122, 165
religion
  of humanity, 87–89, 94, 100, 108–109, 122
  liberal, 104–106, 110, 122, 146–47, 165
religious liberty, 68, 129–32
revelation, 36, 50, 5, 55, 62, 70, 114, 116–17, 134, 141, 144, 151, 155, 157, 159, 161–63